Insight Into Ethiopia

By

Molla Tikuye

xulon PRESS

Copyright © 2009 by Molla Tikuye

Insight Into Ethiopia
by Molla Tikuye

Printed in the United States of America

ISBN 978-1-60647-839-4

All rights reserved solely by the author. The author guarantees all contents are original and do not infringe upon the legal rights of any other person or work. No part of this book may be reproduced in any form without the permission of the author. The views expressed in this book are not necessarily those of the publisher.

Unless otherwise indicated, Bible quotations are taken from The Promise Contemporary English Version. Copyright © American Bible Society, 1995 by Thomas Nelson Inc. and Ethiopian Bible, Old and New Testament, DC R053 printed according to Ethiopian Calendar in 1980 by Ethiopian Bible Association.

www.xulonpress.com

Dedication

The book is dedicated to Our Lord and Savior Jesus Christ, Who is my fortress.....''
Psalm 11:1

Table of Contents   *Page*

Appreciation   11
Forward   12
Introduction   14

Chapter One
Pioneers of Change

Pioneers of Change   20

Chapter Two
Ethiopian History
Through out the Ages

Historical Events Chronological Order   31
Ethiopia since creation of man   38
Ethiopian history for a traveler   40

Chapter Three
Ethiopia & its Uniqueness

Ecology	41
Belief	42
Ethiopia in the Bible	44
Queen of Sheba	46
The Ark	57
The Movement of the Ark in Israel	58
Jaurney of the Ark from Jerusalem to Ethiopia and with in Ethiopia	60
The sketch map of the movement of the Ark from Jerusalem to Ethiopia	62
The Ark in Ethiopia	69
Washington Post & the Ark of Covenant Feb. /10/2002	71
The Stone Tablet	72
Tabernacle of the Lord	72

Chapter Four
Wisdom of Traditional students

Ethiopian Artists	74
Church School Students	
/የቆሉ፡ተማሪ/	74
Mr Tikuye attends traditional school	77
Picture of Traditional Student	78
Wisdom	79
Tikuye the Sculptor	80
Let the Statue speak	81
Introduction of Christianity into Ethiopia	82
Picture of Mr Tikuye	82
Scrolls of Mr Tikuye	84
Writing in Ethiopia	97
A man writing on a Parchment	98
Ancient People	99

Chapter Five
Church and State

Ethiopian Capitals	101
Seek God's leadership	103
God keeps our border	106
National Movement of Fasting and Praying	109
Church's authority over the devil	115
Pray until you touch Heaven	126
Fasting	135
Stand Still	138

Chapter Six
Ethiopia & Tourism

Ethiopia is Peaceful for Tourists	141
Drinking Coffee Together	141
Prehistoric Hominoids Sites	143
Ancient Aksum	143
Lasta – Lalibela	144
Gondar	144
Addis Ababa	145
Thingh a tourist might need to know when looking for Hotels	146
List of Standardized Hotels	147
Reservation – Paper work	148
Checking in	149
Site seeing	151

Temperature	152
Physical Feature	153
Site Seeing in Addis Ababa	156
Signs in the hotels	157
Ethiopians love guests	158
Mount Entoto	159
Ethiopian Culture – religion	159
Respect of elders	160
Injera	161
A farmer plowing	162
Baking Injera	163
Stuffs needed for making Injera	164
Process to bake Injera	165
Food Value of Teff	167
Eating Injera	168
Gursha	169
Ethiopian Calander	172
Ethiopian New Year	172
Months of Ethiopia	174
Days of the Week	175

Chapter Seven

Amharic – Ethiopian Language

Alphabets	176
Amharic Alphabets	176
Ethiopian Consonants	180
Writing in Ethiopian Alphabets	181
Vowels	182
Phonetics	183
Ethiopian Vowels and Consonants	183
Numbers of Ethiopia	184
Languages	190
Ethiopian Alphabets and phonetics	192

Noun	194
Pronoun	194
Body Language	196
Greetings	196
Feminine Difference in Amharic	197
Questions	199
Possessive Pronouns	200
Adjectives	202
Verb – let us	203
Questions	204
Time	208
Shoping Words	209
Punctuations	211
Forms of BE	213
Forms of BE Past Tens	214
Grammar Construction	215
Question forms of:	
a) Is there?	
b) Are there?	219
Numbers ቁጥሮች	221
The Pre-fix which shows ownership	223

Chapter Eight

To practice reading in Amharic

Queen Sheba	224
666 is the Devil itself	226
666 is a scary one	226
Satan is a killer	227
Jesus makes intercession	228
More explanations about life	229
Things one needs to know about God	233

Triad things to know	233
Spiritual Fighting	237
Name of Al – Mighty God	238
Check to be given to those who follow Jesus	240
Salivation – Sinner's Prayer	241
Conclusion	242
Selected Bibliography	244

Appreciation

This book is written in appreciation of Mr. Tikuye's teaching profession and personal gift in art and his love for education. When people neglect agriculture there is a lean harvest. When they neglect education they would suffer from ignorance poverty, and backwardness, because agriculture and education are keys for the development of a nation. In this sense people who give attention for education and agriculture should be appreciated.

Tikuye attended school only for two years in the late 1930's. Becoming a school teacher in Wollo—Ethiopia, he was teaching students from grade 1-8. Going to school for only two years, he was a wonderful teacher of arts, Amharic Grammar, Bible and the ancient language of Geez. Students taught by him witness that he was one of their best teachers they ever had. Some of the students taught by him are internationally well known Sheik Mohammed Hussien Alamoudi and Mr. Melaku Beza- a geologist, Professor Baye Yimam, Engineer Mr. Arega Yirdaw, I and many others still remember him as one of our best teachers.

Sheik Mohammed Hussien Alamoudi and Mr. Melaku Beza thanked Mr. Tikuye recently in a local news paper for teaching them well. Mr. Melaku Beza was really concerned a lot when the school was getting old, worn away and torn into pieces. After constantly thinking what to do with it, he finally shared his concern to Sheik Mohammed Hussien Alamoudi about the matter. So with Melaku's proposal, Sheik Mohammed Hussien Alamoudi rebuilt the school in a magnificient way. Empress Taitu Bitul School, the school where all of us went to learn is found in Wollo/Wldia. The school is named after Empress Taitu Biul because Taitu, the hero who saved Ethiopia from Italian colonization of 1896. She is also popularly known in Ethiopian history as the direct descendant of Ras Ali the Great/ Ras Ali Tiliku.

Mr. Tikuye who is 88 is still mentally cute. He reads the Bible, writes letters to friends and draws pictures without the help of eye glasses.

Molla Tikuye

Forward

I, Molla Tikuye write this book making history my major field of study in Addis Ababa University and then developing experience through teaching history in secondary schools and making researches that ought to be presented in early 1990's for national and international conferences that are held annually under the instruction and guidance of the Institute of Ethiopian Studies and finally after being borne again attending the wonderful Evangelical Church in Washington D.C. for over a decade.

Working with my vision I am happy to come writing this book. I believe that this book would attractive and be beneficial for anyone who reads it. This is because I know from experience as a teacher what boys and girls, ladies and gentlemen; brothers and sisters, adults and yong generation would feel whenever they hear magnificient history of great substance like this.

I have made a lot of researches to find the best material from different books as a miner searches for gold and diamond deep in the ground. So if you read this book it would benefit you esprcially:

* If you have the desire to speak, read and write in Amharic.
* If you are a tourist and want to travel to Ethiopia.
* If you are eager to study ancient, medieval and modern history of Ethiopia.
* if you are an excellent parent, who want to foster Jesus loving children and finally it would help you to raise mentally, physically and psychologically mature children that would someday help their families and their nations. Finally my sincere thanks go to my son, Desalegn Molla who continuously helped me in technical support of the computer.

Some people might think that only males are called

to spread the Word of God. Actually ladies too are called to spread the Word of God. In this connection, I pray for my wife Martha Teklemariam who has a zeal for Jesus to increase her intimacy with Him than ever before and to spread the Word of God far and wide.

According to 2nd Chornithians Chapter 6:1 male or female need to 'work together with Jesus.'' From biblical point of view ladies in particular are assigned by the Lord for the noble mission of spreading the Word, to talk about the resurrection of Jesus, to walk like Jesus and to live like Jesus. Take for example the three women who discovered the empty tomb on Mark 16:6.Disappointed but never been despaired, the first people to go to the tomb of Jesus on the third day of His death were the three women, who were His real friends. Today also real friends of Jesus expect His second coming singing the song of Maranatha.

When the three women discovered at first the empty tomb they were really alarmed. When they were excited the the angel of the Lord told them:'' Don't be alarmed, you are looking for Jesus of Nazareth, who was nailed to the Cross. God has raised Him to life. He is not here. (See: Marks 16:6,) Go your way. Tell His disciples and Peter that He goes before you into Galilee. (See Mark 16:7) This shows that every body who accepts Jesus as his Savior is assigned to spread the Word of God. Presented in a historiographic form the mission of this book form is to encourage righteous brothers and sisters to spread the Word of God.

Introduction

Historiography, the record of human life and society helps us study man in the past and present and consequently to foresee the future. Because history helps to foresee the future, I write this book to initiate the young generation study culture, language, socio-political affairs, religion of their ancestors and particularly of their history because it is one of the great humanities that broadens the horizon of young generation. So since it is important to teach history for any one starting from age eight until he is eighty, this would help young generation comprehend national, international, political, social, religious and cultural arenas.

Since history prepares young generation to be leaders, governors, lawyers and statesmen, I have written lots of history in this book to teach rights, responsibilities and obligations of people in the society. In this book, I have also written Ethiopia's development, challenges and prospectives and from the perspective of history & politico-religious.

When I was in Ethiopia/Wollo/ Woldia I was eager to know the ancient and the present history of Ethiopia. The soil, the people and all the sites in Wollo/ Woldia tell history. So when I was a young child in Woldia I had the desire to study history. Working with it I achieved what I wanted. I have collected history of the area from many elder oral informants or shimagilewoch /ሽማግሌዎች/ in Amharic. These elders were notables of their community and communual elders from historical perspective.

As time passed by, however; I hear that most of my elder oral informants have passed away. So whenever I hear news about their death, I become sorry, because I consider these elders as great history tellers and as my big history libraries. This is because it was due to the feed back of these oral informants that I have a good historical knowledge about Ethiopia. Now I can do nothing about these elders. What I can do now is to transfer their legacy to the next generation. Hence if there is any body willing to know history I am ready to share what I heard from oral informants and what I read from books and from what I was taught in schools and in Addis Ababa University .

I have also included in this book Ethiopian culture, Amharic alphabets, words, phrases and sentences thinking that all these materials would help some one learn about Ethiopian way of life and also Amharic, the official Ethiopian language.

Young generation born outside of Ethiopia but were originally from Ethiopia, if they don't pay attention to the writing system, culture and history of their ancestors they would fail to trace their origin with the elapse of time. But before that, learning Amharic and history can save them from this imminent problem. Concerned with this matter, this book has come with a solution. Since the problem is a big one the solution for the problem is open for public attention.

In America there are foreign language institutes in different states, cities and counties. These institutes help especially those students who speak predominant languages of Spanish, French, Chinese, Japanese, Korean, Indian, Arabic, etc.... However; it does not seem to help much Amharic speakers.

Even though; Amharic is the language of all Ethiopians and is also one of the major languages in America; experts of foreign language institute in America believe that languages like Amharic are not given attentionas much as Spanish, Arabic, Japanese or Chinese. According to their belief Amharic is not a business language like the Chinese, the Japanese, and Spanish or like the Arabic. Since population of Ethiopia in America as compared to Chinese, Japanese, Arabs of Middle East and Spanish is low, Foreign Language departments do not pay much attention to foreign students who want to practise their native language. They just help these people to improve their English. In the mean time however; kids with Ethiopian origin should not be left alone when they want to use their language.

Eventhough; teaching kids is a family business

and home is the first place where teaching should begin, some parents, however; neglect to teach their kids. If that is the case, Sunday school programs are good for such a family like this. A good family should not, however; depend on Sunday school teachers for their kids. What goes around comes around. Since teaching kids is a natural parental thing they have to teach their kids themselves or find a solution for them.

    This book does not fill this gap completely. But to a certain degree it will fill up a small vaccum to help kids in their effort to study Amharic and Bible.

    Thinking that it will also quench childrens' thirst to know the history of their country, I have come with this book to teach them right from wrong and when you teach the youth the long term expectation for your kids is bright according to Prov. 22:6.

''Teach your children right from wrong.
When they are grown up they will still do right.''Prov.22:6.
This means:

"ልጅህን፡በሚሄድበት፡መንገድ፡ምራው፡፡
በሽመገለም፡ጊዜ፡ከዕርሱ፡ፈቀቅ፡አይልም፡፡"
(ምሳሌ፡22፡ቁጥር፡6)

    To teach a child right from wrong is easy. If the parent helps him in his home work and follows the progress of his child he will be a brilliant stdent for the rest of his life. If the parent tells his child to believe and trust in the Lord, God will do the rest on his behalf. If the parent teaches his child one of the foreign languages especially English he can live anywhere in the world. If he teaches him just only Amharic or Oromigna he can not survive outside of Ethiopia. On your behalf teach your kid every thing good for him. After that according to Proverb 3:2, the child will lead a prosperous life for the rest of his life. The reason why Emperor Haile Selassie I became brilliant is because his father helped him a lot in his home.

''Insight into Ethiopia'' refers to the historiography and cultural heritage of Ethiopia, a country located in north-east Africa. The title is given to this book because this country of the Horn has lots of history, Ark, Script and historical sites as you will see later. In the next paragraphs we are also going to see the emergence and development of Amharic as a language of script.

Amharic is one of the major Semitic languages. Semites were the descendants of Shem. According to Genesis 10:1, Shem was one of the three sons of Noah. As one of the major Semitic languages, Amharic helps to write fiction, poetry, literature, history, bible, and that is because it has got a wonderful script.

Ethiopia the oldest African country uses Amharic as a language of script for centuries. The two Semitic brothers, namely; Tigray and Amhara speak Tigrigna and Amharic respectively and this shows that the two languages are similar Semitic languages because both of them come from the same root.

The role of Amharic in Ethiopia is nothing but to make the bond of relationship among the peoples of Tigray, Eritrea, Oromos, the Ethiopian ninety tribes and races of the world to be very strong. So as a unifying factor the Amharic language has moulded and shaped the unity of the Ethiopian people. Apart from that in the sphere of administration Amharic has been popularly used as the sole official dominant language of Ethiopia for hundreds of years.

Wherever man lives there is history. On the land where God made land, man setltled down, built villages and statrted history.Ethiopia is one of these places. Man has lived in Ethiopia since time of immemorial. Because man has live in Ethiopia since early times there is a lot of history. The problem of newly emerging countries is their scant early history. But the problem of Ethiopia is too much early and present history. Because of this rich historical resource has accumulated and is now difficult to handle. Due to therefore; her historical reputation and too much history the eye of the world has always been on Ethiopia. For this reason many people from the outside world try day and night to discover what man was doing in the past in Ethiopia.

In the old good days and good ways of the middle Ages the occident the western world was looking for Ethiopia. So they were asking travellers of the time where this marvelous country was located on the map. In particular the occident in those ages were searching for the Christian king whose name they called ''Prester John''was located.

After-hardly-discovering-Ethiopia, Europeans started to send more travellers to make a frequent contact with Ethiopia effective. One of these early travellers of 18th century who found out more information about Ethiopia was James Bruce. After him more travellers and missionaries continued to flow into Ethiopia and all their works is well documented in history books.

I give the title, ''Insight into Ethiopia'' to this book for the purpose of making the content overwhelming and helpful to travellers and for any one who might be interested to know about Ethiopia. For that matter I have included Ethiopian history, culture, Amharic alphabets, Amharic words, phrases and sentences thinking that all these materials would help some one learn Amharic with out a teacher. Amharic derives from the ancient language, Geez. So Amharic helps to understand socio-politics, history, Christianity and Ethiopian religious books that were written in Geez and then were translated to Amharic. What has been said above is a clue and this might help people to make research.

For those who plan to make research about Ethiopia, Amharic helps a lot, because it has got outstanding script. Amharic is one of the major languages. Had it not been a major language, I couldn't have been motivated to pick up a pen and pad to write about it. So far what has been written might have given you a hint. Since the book is written for the glory and deication of the Lord, I thank Jesus, my Lord and Savior, in every thing He does in my life and for helping me write this book.

   <u>N.B:</u>- At the end of writing this book, the need to use Portable Document Format (PDF) files was necessary. But when using Power Ge'ez font, the 6th letter of the Amharic alphabet (ኢ) was not recognized in the PDF. In the same tokn the 4th letter of the Amharic letter of (ቷ) was not recognized in the PDF we used in this book. Because of this problem we have used the 6th letter of the Amharic alphabet (0). Also as to the question of the 4th letter of the Amharic alphabet (ቷ) we have used (ቷኢ) in some pages of the book. So please make a note of this problem. We are sorry about the inconvience.

Chapter 1

Pioneers of change

For the sake of bright future of Ethiopian young generation, Emperor Haile Selassie beginning from the initial time he came to power and while he was in power worked hard to foster great Ethiopian generation. For this reason his education policy was based on ''how to mould the young generation.''

To hit on the target of his plan, because he was a wise man he at first observed European interest in Ethiopia. Then after observing and fully comprehending European motive, he visited Europe officially in 1924. [See''My life and the Ethiopian Progress biography:/'ሀይወቴና:የኢትዮጵያን:ርምጃ/''page 63.]

The book''My life and the Ethiopian Progress/'ሀይወቴና የኢትዮጵያን ርምጃ/ written by the Emperor himself illustrates his great love of the two inseparable elements of education and young generation. Though he was not highly educated, he was working hard to see others educated. As a young boy he was the beloved son of his father Ras Mekonnen and also Menilik II, who was Emperor of Ethiopia towards the end of the nineteen century and the beginning of the twentieth century.

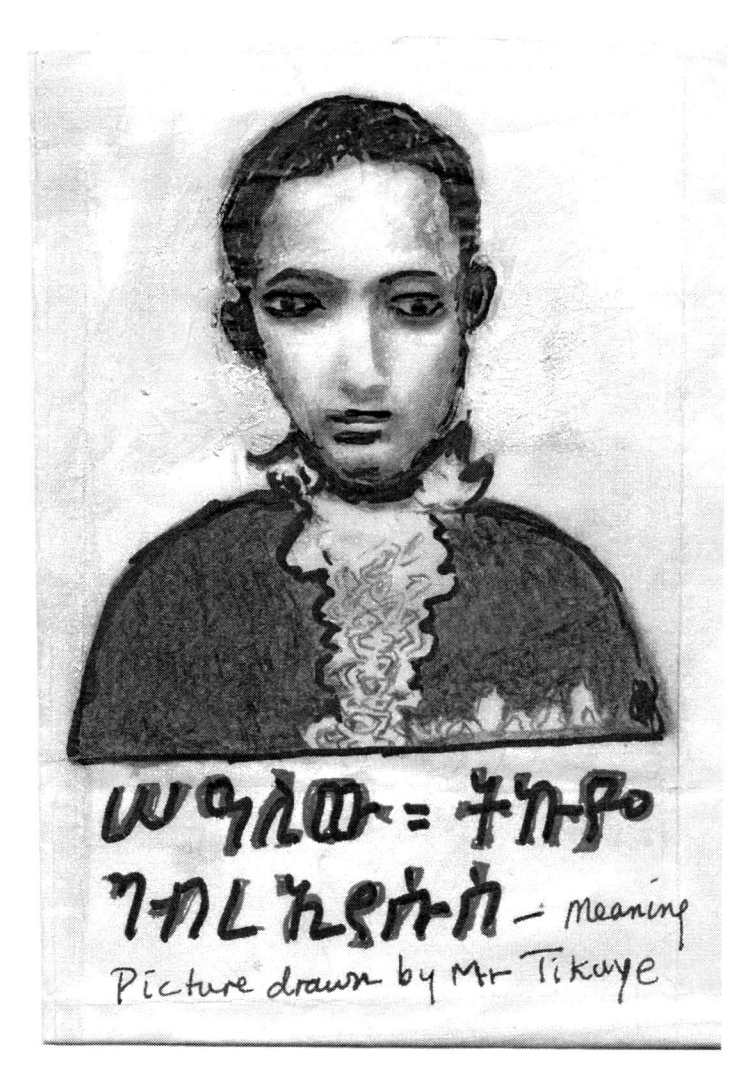

ሠዓሊው = ትክክም
ግብር እያሱህ – meaning
Picture drawn by Mr Tikuye

Picture of Emperor Haile Selassie when he was twelve years old

     While Emperor Haile Selassie I was a young boy he was called Teferi. It was in 1905 that Teferi at the age of 13 became governor of a region in Harer. In 1906 his father Ras Mekonen was sick. When he was sick his father was worried not because of his own death but of his little boy's fortune with out a father and a mother for his mother had died while he was toddler. Nonetheless; he consigned little Teferi to Emperor Menilik II to his care, mentioning in the next life he would ask him how he raised his son, the little Teferi.

Source: Haile SelassieI – The Formative Years 1892 - 1936 by Harold Marcus page 5-6.

I mention Emperor Haile Selassie I so that the young generation would aspire to be great leaders, nationalists and elite of the future. As a young boy Teferi Mekonnen had never spent a single day drinking, loitering or even playing with his peer group. While he was a small boy, eventhough, he was with out father and mother; he was going up in the ladder of success and power from time to time.

Simultaneously while growing in power and fame he was simultaneously drafting important schemes of development and modernization for his country because his sole desire was to see growth and development of the new and modern Ethiopia. So to fulfill his program of modernization for his beloved country he visited Europe in 1924. All this information comes from the documents that the Emperor wrote himself.

How wonderful it is when leaders themselves write their own biography. When leaders write about themselves real history is written. Take for example the biography of Harry Truman. It was written by him. If you get the chance to read it read it. It is wonderful. Take also the biography of Emperor Haile Selassie I. It was written by the Emperor himself. It is marvelous and sweet to read. When one finds that the book is sweet and marvelous, he might think that the Emperor was highly educated. According to his biography, however; because the Emperor wrote the reality about his educational background we understand that he was not highly educated.

Though he was not highly educated and though he was too young, his achievement in socio-econo-geo-political-religeous, and other governmental affairs as a little boy was marvelous. Every thing he did was a surprise. Every thing he did was also in an excellent way because of his natural gift and brilliance. This was because Ras Mekonnen, his father was taking care of him as a young boy. For further illustration read what is written here below.

Emperor Haile Selassie's biography is recorded by Harold Marcus, the American historian who translated the biography of Emperor Haile Selassie I into English. Harold Marcus loves and appreciates the Emperor because the Emperor was not only wise but was also a man of strategy. According to the belief of Emperor Haile Selassie what must be done first must be done first. So as a man of strategy, before laying down a program to develop Ethiopia because he was wide in outlook he at first visited Europe planning to expand education and to excel Europeans in science and technology. According to a certain book; '' How Japan becomes Civilized? I read this while young but the idea is put in my memory. According to this book, ''Ethiopia under Emperor Haile Selassie I was trying to develop very fast. But it is alleged that due to the interference of external powers the progress of Ethiopia curtailed short. As you know the political terms like internal relations and external relations has an impact upon a given country. Since Ethiopia is not immune from this global effect, you will learn a lot if you scan through through international political affairs.

In spite of the obstacles he faced beginning from the time the Emperor returned from Europe he was continuously sending Ethiopian young students abroad for further academic studies, scientific discoveries, to study the culture of the West, the English language and much more. In those days Emperor

Haile Selassie I had established great diplomatic relationship with Europe and America. Because of that he initiated Ethiopian students to go to the West to study the English language, Western culture and education. This was because he believed that learning English and Western culture were key factors necessary to modernize Ethiopia.

On the other hand Emperor Haile Selassie I did not forget those young children who were handicap, mentally ill, the orphanage, and others who were needy in his time. He believed that the mentally ill, the orphans and the handicapped young generation can succeed in life and contribute their part for their nation. So he helped such children a lot opening schools, giving incentives or rewards, visiting them personally and talking to them individually. Because he was interested in theyoung generation, he used to visit their dinning rooms, tasting their dinner and encouraging the management to feed the kids fruits and vegetables/አትክልት/ daily, beef wott /የበሬ ስጋ/ rarely and chicken wott /ዶሮ ወጥ/ weekly. Those of us, who went to Haile Selasie I University and those of us who were educated at that time are witness. We were educated in the campass free of charge enjoying the delicious food, the libraries, recreation centers, and other facilities of this wonderful and internationally accredited huge university. In the beginning all the site and all the buildings of the present day University which is located in Sidit Kilo was the former palace and personal property of the Emperor himself. But due to his love of his country and the young generation the Emperor gave his palace to the people of Ethiopia so that they can use it as a university. Granting his land and the land he received from his father, Ras Mekonnen to the people of Ethiopia was not a one time occasion. He had granted land of his own several times to open new schools. For example the land where Teferi Mekonnen Secondary school was built was at first granted by Emperor Haile Selassie I himself.

Emperor Haile Selassie I like to speak with handicap children because he believes that such handicap children have a lot to contribute for their country. He also used to treat every child equally. He did not care whether the child was from central, northen, southern, eastern or western Ethiopia. This was therefore the reason why every kid in the country loved him a lot and was singing the school sonng popularly known'' Ababa Janihoy, our father and mother, has raised us feeding honey and milk.'' Meaning in Amharic:

"አባባ፡ ጃንሆይ፡የኛ፡ዕናት፡አባት።
አሳድገውናል፡ በማር፡ በወተት።"

Every body educated in his time was singing this this song in the schools and in his home. No student seems to be exceptional, though many of us turned against his rule later on and of course for giving our back to him we have paid the price.

ሥዕሉ፡ ተስሎ፡ ገቢር፡ እየሉት
ዘቲኩይ፡ ኢትዮጵ — meaning -
picture drawn by Tikuye - who is Ethiopian in nationality

The picture above drawn by Mr. Tikuye shows a girl who can not see. She is talking with the Emperor, because the Emperor believes that such handicap children have a lot to contribute for their country.

This in Amharic means

"በንጉሥ፡ነገሥቱ፡ ዕምነት፡አይነ - ስውራን፡ ለሀገራቸው፡ የሚያበረክቱት፡ ብዙ ነገር፡ አለ።"

Emperor Haile I was doing all this to help the young generation. If you want to verify this you can refer the book entitled: " ንጉሥ፡ነገሥቱ፡" - written by Getachew Mekonnen

Hasen in 1984 Ethiopian calendar Addis Ababa , pages 137-138, 149- 150. Because of his love for
young generation Emperor Haile Selassie I was known as:" Father of Education." Pending this for a while, let us talk about what must be done for the next generation.

Unless one holds a master key in his hands, he can't enter into the rooms of an apartment complex. Same thing is true if one does not know the language of other people he can not talk with other people. Language not only helps to establish relationship, but also assists to transmit heritage from forefathers to the succeeding generations.

Ethiopian ancestors had introduced the young generation with the West, Near East, Middle East and the Far East. To communicate with all these countries they sent us to schools to learn English.

Our ancestors protected our country from invaders. They sent us to schools to learn major world languages so that we can communicate with the whole world. So the generation is greatful to them; though, there is a lot to be done in return. We have to follow their foot step. Especially those who were educted in Ethiopia and those who have got power and money need to bring change.

After being born, raised and educated in the mother land but forgetting the soil of ancestors and sitting idle is not good. One can serve the country where he resides and his/ her original homeland at the same time. There is nothing wrong in this. Leave alone those who were born on the soil of their ancestors, world population is becoming one community. One can not exhaust mentioning the names of those ouside people who help Ethiopia. This is not to under estimate the continual struggle of Ethiopians who were born on the soil of Ethiopia or abroad. Take for example the history of people like Nagadras Gabra Hiwat Baykadan.Of course it is hardly possible mentioning the names of such people. For you convenience you can read the paper of Professor Bahru which he wrote on:" Pioners of change in Ethiopia."

To mould a child's growth and development we

have to tell the young generation about pioneers of change in schools and in our homes. This is because people who were important in the past are our model today. Look at America which had and is having leaders of change. Take for example George Washington, President Kennedy who was people of change. The name of these men is mentioned because they are excellent model. This is the type of leader that a country needs today. It was George Washington who brought bright future for America fighting for independence and freedom. Today people in America still love ''George Washington ''because Washington worked hard to make America great. Indeed George Washington was a popular American president. He was elected for two terms in the last quarter of the 18th century. With out exaggeration he had worked for the bright future of America and for the victory of the American War of Independence. Winning the war he brought freedom for his people and popularity for himself. Because of this today George Washington is known as the man: ''... first in war, first in peace, and first in the hearts of his country men.'' He was born on February 22, 1732 in Virginia. – Source- Grolier Inc.MCMXCIV.

One cannot necessarily need to hold a high post to make history. Any person can be a great man if he has got the gut. Take for example people like Senator Barack Obama. In the case of our country Ethiopia on the other hand, we should not forget our history. When I was studying for my Bachelor's degree, Professor Bahru a professor who loves his country was teaching more about the contribution of Ethiopian foreign students like Nagadras Gabra Hiwat Baykadan, an intellectual who contributed a lot for a change in Ethiopia.

According to Professor Bahru, Nagadras Gabra Hiwat Baykaddan was born in Adawa on July 30/ 1886. He lived in the time of Emperor Menilik II and Emperor Haile Selassie I. It was in his early childhood that he managed to go to Europe. After he completed his studies he came back to Ethiopia.Then he contributed a lot to Ethiopia. Soon after he came back to Ethiopia he studied Amharic. He studied how to read and write. With in seven months he finished every thing he wanted to learn about Amharic language. Then he started to write in Amharic. He was known as the finest writer of Amharic prose.

Though he short lived from July 30/ 1886 to July 1/ 1919 living only 33 years, his work is still in memory of Ethiopian people. It is pity sometimes death takes away the best leaving behind the weak and the feeble. Ethiopia had lost brilliant people many times. She lost her intellectuals in the 1930's when Italian Fascism massacred the emerging intellectuals of Ethiopia. Again Ethiopia lost her intellectuals due to the infiltration of communism in 1970's and in 1980's.

Young children always expect some thing from the old dying generation. So the old generation must always be ready to leave some thing behind for the next generation. A good child growth and development is very important to the development of a nation and for the survival of a good family; though a good family is the nucleus and basic foundation to raise brilliant children.

For a reason that cannot be expressed in words, but is instinct, natural, inborn and real parents naturally love their kids. Parents while they suffer from hard life they give priority for their kids. While they are illiterate they send their kids to best schools. While they wear casual clothes they buy best suits for their children. This portays for a good child growth and development home is important. Mostly, home, especially sweet home is crucial for parenting the best child in the best possible way. The role of the government for best child growth and development should not also be neglected. In either case sensible instruction of a person in his/her early stage is highly important. The Bible supports this, it says: "A sensible instruction is a life-giving fountain that helps you escape all deadly traps." Prov.13:14

Child growth and development is a natural process. In Child growth and development there is growth and change in the anatomy and physiology of a child. This change is from simple to complex. It is when nature changes the child that he/ she will become an adult. Child growth and development is not; however, quick. It needs patience. Animals have no problem. They grow fast. In a few days or weeks they can be independent of their parents. Unfortunately, man is dependent up on his parents for unlimited time.

Though; the process of change is not easy, if family network is good, there will be a conducieve condition to raise a good child that will change into normal adulthood. Good child rearing needs joint parenting of both the father and the mother. Rarely, however; a single strong father or mother can also raise a good child.

If a determined family raises a child in good condition starting from the diaper stage to the beginning of the adolescent age, there will be no reason why a good parent will not have a good kid. So if the family remain good through out, the kid will also be good through out. But if the family is broken, the chance of the kid to be a good citizen will be geopardized.

Take Ethiopia a traditional society for example. In traditional Ethiopia family value is very important with some exceptions. In Ethiopia a child stays together with his family working with the father or with the mother in his/ her spare time. So when the child stays together with the family, the child develops an excellent behavior and a good experience of work in the household or in the field.

I know an Ethiopian who took his son from America to Ethiopia after observing that his kid was involved in some kind of bad behavior. Sometimes it is good to get experience from developing societies or from back home. So if you are an Ethiopian, take your child to Ethiopia and show him how people live over there. If you are an American take him for a trip to one of the developing countries. After you take him for a trip, when he returns home, your child will not be the same. He will be a different child learning news things and understanding what real life looks like.

Moreover; going together, eating together and doing things together with your kid is one of the important factors for raising a good child. This is because by doing things together with your child, you will develop not only warm relationship with your child but also it will be a good time for your child to create a good vision of becoming a good child. When raising your kid please let him to rationalize facts by him. So in this case parents should avoid imposing in the child's mind their own views,

because the child needs freedom to think and by himself and develop his independent life.
    Kids of Ethiopian origin, but born outside should know the language of their ancestors. Plus when people from other lands show the interest to learn Amharic we should have available materials. So if you consider this book to be worthy for your children it is available for you.

Chapter 2
Historical Events in Chronological Order

It is lovely when one studies history in chronological order. Down here you are going to read Ethiopian history in chronological order. In history Ethiopia is known as museum of history. In geography it is known as an ancient country located in North-east Africa, between longitudes 30 and 48 degrees east and latitudes 3 and 18 degrees north.

Historically Ethiopia is an old timer. It is also a country of all time independent. It is populated and over cultivated through out the last four or five millennia. But still the soil is just fertile. Today it is populated next to Nigeria and Egypt. It is generally known as the Horn of Africa, because of the horn shaped tip of the continent that marks the Red Sea from the Indian Ocean according to history and reality.

It is lovely when one studies history in chronological order because when one studies history in sequence of events it is easy to understand. All the time studying any subject from simple to complex widens the realm of his knowledge. Since I am major in history I know too many facts and dates. So I have prepared the following note for you to explain Ethiopian history from the earliest times to the present. As a history teacher I have put it in chronological order as follows.

1st - At first animal and plant domestication might have started in Ethiopia between 4000 &1000 B.C. The Ethiopian staple food, teff might have started with in this time. We know that civilization in ancient times started near river valleys. If this prehistory is true then domestication of plants and animals might have started in Ethiopia in the Lower Nile valley or around Awash River as far as I believe. The first domesticated plant in Ethiopian history is really unknown. While I was a teacher in Ethiopia I taught students that '' Enset, the staple food of the tribe of Guraghe '' grew in 4000 B.C. I got that information in 9th grade history text. According to another history text the staple food of Ethiopia ''teff, '' first grew along the banks of the Blue Nile in Gojjam region. Land in

Ethiopia is still tilled with oxen. The people of Ethiopia are very smart. There are many scientists all over the globe. But for an unknown reason land ploughing tecknique has not shown a break through. This being the reason lean harvest and hunger of Ethiopia needs an immediate slution.

A man tilling his land with his oxen to sow teff- staple food of Ethiopia

      Ethiopia is one of the few places of the world where early man started agriculture. If plants are near river and man is near to God Al-Mighty there is no problem. These days in particular mankind in general in every part of the world suffers when he fails to trust the Lord. In the same token plants suffer drought when there is no available water. The further explanation of this follows here with.

      In Ethiopia along the banks of the Blue Nile Gorge plants and animals produce fruit very easily because of the fertile soil and water of the Abbay River / or the Blue Nile. Since creation of the earth plants growing on fetile soil and animals grazing on grass along/ or near both banks of Abbay have never faced any shortage of water and/ or silt of soil. In the same token those who come close to God Al-Mighty do not face hunger and starvation because according to Psalm 23 God fills their cups until overflow. To get such type of previledge of course a man or a woman has to refuse sin and evil advice. For such people since the creation of the earth / or ever since the Old Testament according to the Book of Psalms Chapter one, the Law of the Lord makes them happy and rich because these people think about the Word of God day and night.

According to the Book of John1:1, the faith of such people is the Word. They believe that the Word is truly God and just due to their faith they always produce more fruit. Where water is there is life. Water is also symbol of Holy Spirit. Plants which grow near a river get plenty of water and rich fertile soil. In the same token people who come close to God live in a place of safety and protection according to ''Psalm 91:1-2''

2nd-Next Pre-Axumite Period might have started between the 3rd millennium B.C. and 10th century A. D. In the same token according to the history of the people of Israel Period of Exodus was between 2nd millennium B.C. and 13th Century B.C. It is good to know dates. Many books give clues when events happened in the bible. The author of the Old Testament B.W. Anderson who writes about the Old Testament for example explains when events happened in the Bible. On the other hand almost all history books explain when events happened in the history of mankind. In general it is good to know when events happened.

With out knowing dates and the location of the historical place it is hardly possible to fully comprehend both the the Bible and history. By 1350 B.C. we remember Moses, an important figure in the period of Exodus. We also learn that the Ark of the Covenant was built in 1350 BC. In the years around 1000 B.C. we remember King David. King Solomon lived and ruled in Israel. Queen Sheba was queen of Ethiopia in 950 B.C. Queen Sheba is contemporary to King Solomon. Thus it was in the time of Queen Sheba and King Solomon that blood link between Ethiopia and Israel started and it was this blood relationship that paved the way for the establishment of the Solomon Dynasty in

Ethiopia. When relationship is based upon political interest the bond of relationship is not strong. When relationship is built on the basis of blood the relationship is strong. This was why the relationship between Ethiopia and Israel was strong for three thousand years.

3rd - Queen Sheba and King Solomon gave birth to Menilik I in 950 B. C. The religious and political relationship between Israel in Jerusalem and Ethiopia in Aksum at that time was hot. When the relationship was strong the Ark of the Covenant came into Ethiopia. The Ark came to Ethiopia by 950 B.C. In the later chapter you will see how the Ark came from Israel to Ethiopia. Of course it was as a result of the hot relationship between Israel and Ethiopia in the Aksumite the Ark of the Covenant was able to come to Ethiopia. But pending this for a while let us view or review about the chronological events of Ethiopia since the Creation of man and major events since the Birth of Jesus.

The Ark of the Covenant- the original golden Ark that was made in the time of Moses and that which was 36 inches long, 18 inches wide and 26 inches high according to the Book of Exodus Chapter 25: 23-25

4th - Jesus came into the world to be the Saviour of all people according to the Book of Luke. Of course according to the Bible it was between B.C. & A.D. that Jesus was born. The end of B.C. and the beginning of A.D. is the beginning of God's grace to mankind. It is called:-" The New Testament." This is why since the birth of Jesus we celebrate Christmas, the greatest Holy Day in the history of mankind. From Adam to Moses, from Moses to Solomon and from King Solomon to Jesus there was no any just man to take away our sin. It was the fulfillment of the promise of God. The first promise of God is Genesis 3:15. According to the Lord's promise Jesus sent by God, born in about 1 A. D. from Virgin Mary took away our sin.

According to John Wesley, Jesus came with the Gospel to save us-: It was a thing unheard before; a virgin should conceive and bear a son! But by the power of the Holy Spirit Immanuel was born in Bethelehem. Immanuel means - God with us (See: Matt. 1:23.) Immanuel is with us in weakness and poverty according to Spurgeon – (See Spurgeon - Morning &Evening from page 732-33)

5th - Christianity was introduced into Ethiopia in 344 A.D. Soon after Christianity was introduced a beautiful Church called "New Covenant Tsion" was built in Axum. According to the Book of Ethiopis it took seventeen years to build the Church. It was built out of silver, diamond and gold according to early Ethiopian biblical history. For your surprise the name "New Covenant Tsion" shows the strong belief of early Ethiopians in God Al-Mighty and their honour of Tsion.

6th - By 12th Century A.D, the Lalibela Rock Churches were built in Ethiopia especially in the city of Lasta in Wollo province. The rock–hewn Church of Lasta is the 8th wonder of the world. The Temple of Solomon is the 7th wonder of the world.

7th - Gondar became the capital of Ethiopia between 13th Century and 17th Century A.D.

8th - Addis Ababa was built in 1880's. Since its foundation it has been the capital city of Ethiopia.

9th - The beginning of modernization might have started in Ethiopia by 900.

10th - Between 1935-1941 Italy interfered in the internal affairs of Ethiopia

11th - Ethio-British diplomacy was between 1941-- 1960.

12th - Ethio-America diplomacy was from 1960 to early 1970's.

13th - About 226 kings claiming descent from the of the Solmon line ruled in Ethiopia

The last of the 226th kings that ruled in Ethiopia claiming his descent to the Solmon line is Emperor Haile Selassie I. The Emperor, however; who was the consolidator and modernizer of the empire was killed secretly by the pressure of the Russian aetheists and by the instigation of the puppets and power mongers of Ethiopia in 1974.

Emperor Haile Selassie I

14th - The philosophy of Socialism was written by Marx, Engels and Lenin. These three men were philosophers of Socialism in Russian history. Russia interfered in the internal affairs of Ethiopia from 1974 to 1991. Socialism disrupted the rule of the Solomon dynasty and although Socialism introduced aetheism into Ethiopia, people gave a deaf ear to such a philosophy. Theoritically the philosophy of Socialism seemed good. Practically however; there was no fruit.

Picture of Marx, Engels and Lenin
   When Ethiopia was under Communism people were fed up of frequent meetings and lots of contribution. So people expressed their hatred in different ways. Take for example what the people said herewith.

Three brothers one of them is bald.
Organize meetings, people to attend
But ask money at every meeting & that isn't good.

Ethiopia – Since Creation of Man

Though Ethiopia is not part of the Middle East, it is very close to the Mediterranean World, the Middle East and the Garden of Eden. Because Ethiopia is near the Middle East her faith is based on monotheism. Geographically the Bible tells us that the second river that flows from the Garden of Eden is Gihon. According to the Bible Gihon is a river that winds through Ethiopia. (See Genesis 2:10-14.) Ethiopia calls the Ghion River the Blue Nile. The people of Ethiopia call it Abbay River. In Ethiopia there are songs about Abbay River. The Tis - Isat in the Abbay Valley is like the Niagara Falls. Abbay in Ethiopia and Niagara Falls of North America are wonderful tourist sites.

The Bible which teaches about the beginning of creation tells us that man was created in the Garden of Eden. This truth does not change. The record of the Bible does no change. This is because what is already documented in the Bible is not information or fact, but truth. Truth does not change with time. What is documented in the Bible is the Word of God and the Word of God is Jesus and what is from Jesus does not change. He is in charge of what is written in the Bible. He is Alpha & Omega and what He said in the Bible is Alpha & Omega too.

So far with the exception of Jesus nobody has a clear understanding of the Bible. For example reading the Bible nobody with the exception of Jesus knows how man spread from the Garden of Eden to other parts of the world. Presumably Ethiopia, being very close to the Garden of Eden and its Gihon flowing from Eden might have been one of the early man's habitations. Today modern man using sophisticated technology is eager to know early man's history. So to make research about early man a lot of money is being spent from time to time.

Though it is by digging the ground, archaeology is the study of early man. It is one of the branches of history which denies theory of Creation tells us too much information about early man. Information of archaeology changes constantly. Because of its constant change of information archeaeology still searches for more information and still its information is unrealible.

Though; archaeology and Bible have different ways to investigate the history of man, both of them agree that Ethiopia is one of the oldest countries on earth. For a believer in God the material from the Bible is true and reliable. However; archaeologists still lose money, time and energy to prove for mankind that they have a better knowledge. To one's surprise they are digging grounds in the different sites of Ethiopia, whose people believe in Creation.

In Ethiopia archaeologists dig places in search of early history. So tourists have a good chance to visit historical sites of early man. Lucy or Dinki-nesh is the 1st longest human remains in the world. The remnant was discovered in a place called Hidar in Wollo in Ethiopia. The archeologists who discovered this evidence were happy on the day they discovered. On that evening while celebrating day of their joy they were listening to the song, 'Lucy in the Heavens'. It was after listening to the song they agreed to call the remains of the bone Lucy. The archeologist also told us this information in one of the classes when we were taking one of archaeology courses. Wollo is my birth place. The archaeologist was my lecturer. This is why I tell you the story precisely. Bible is my wonderful book. Though Wollo is my birth place and the archaeologist is my lecturer I strongly believe in creation. You too have a choice. Truth is from God Al-Mighty. Evolution is from Darwin and this is the truth.

Ethiopian History for a traveler

As a traveler one always wants to know where he is heading and what type of people he is going to visit. If you are going to visit Ethiopia you are going to see an old historical country known as a museum of history in Africa. You are going to a beautiful country of thirteen months of sunshine. You are going to visit a place with many terrains and low lands. The high terrains are really high and the lowlands are really low. The low land is found in the Danakil Depression. Here there are places as low as over 100 meters below sea level and is believed to be the lowest sea level in the world. The highlands of Ethiopia are really high. There are places as high as 4500 meters above sea level. In between the high mountains and the low lands you have rivers, plains, mountains and series of lakes in the Rift Valley of Ethiopia.

In Ethiopia you visit lots of historical sites and artifacts. You visit sites of the evolution of man. You visit many Churches and monasteries. If you want to see the evolution of early man in Ethiopia, you are going to see the evolution of Hominoids in the Pre-historic period, which began with the emergence of Hominoids of the Australopithicus.

Pre-historic time is the Pre- Axumite time. No matter what! Either way, through evolution or through Creation, Ethiopia is one of the 1st inhabited places in the world. Because it is one of the 1st inhabited places, it is one of the 1st countries of the world which has a recorded history. For that matter; Ethiopia is one of the oldest countries with civilization. The gravity of the centre of advanced civilization was in ancient Axum. As a civilized place there is evidence that coins were minted in Axum.

There are many new things in Ethiopia and therefore it is known in African studies as the cliché' of unique things. As a matter of fact therefore if one goes to the Omo valley, he would find new things. If he gose to the high Semein Mountain, he would find unique things. I just jot down all this from what I know as a history teacher. And in a real sense more than what is written in this book Ethiopia is of course rich in history.

Chapter 3
Ethiopia and its uniqueness

Ecology

Ethiopia which is a unique country believes in Al-Mighty God, and that God of the Bible. It is also a country of unique physical geographic feature, animals and plants. There are many species of animals and plants unique in Ethiopia. In general is Ethiopia is a country of endemic animals and plants. Endemic means – plants or animals that exist on the surface of the earth. Ethiopia is a country of endemic plants and animals. Ethiopia has got a unique place in Africa studies because there are many unique things. Some of them of these unique features are: the belief in Trinity [triune nature of God or the Sostu Silassie as it is called in Ethiopia, Gibir system, or (the land holding system), the Tabot Christianity or (Ark of Covenant), the Axumite civilization, and the culture of eating the special bread, engera, the unique animals the alphabets and the Ethiopian calendar. Also if you watch National Geography Channel, you will see many unique things in Ethiopia. Take for example Erta Ale Lava Lake of the Afar region, which has the most powerful and active volcano in the world. A unique thing helps to make more research. So researchers should continue their research on the Erta Ale Lava Lake of the Afar region, because if the volcano oozes out in the future it would have a global effect.

Nowadays in particular because of deforestation, population pressure and due to negligence, plants and animals die in Ethiopia than ever before. Especially these days a significant number of species of plants are being lost every year. If you are a geneaologist of plants you can do much better. You know more about climate change. You also know that and number of plants and animals are becoming extinct. From my personal assessment this book gives you a tip about two endemic plants. So you want to make further research on the plants mentioned herewith before they are lost completely.

1) Presumably there might be some unique plants in Wollo, Yejju. In Yejju – In Wollo/ Woldia research has not been done on these unique plants in general. If you go there farmers will tell you. A unique legume by the name Agerie ater which costs three times than other legumesand that is rich in protein seems endemic to Wollo/ Ethiopia.
2) The other plant endemic to Yejju / Wollo is Marchigie or Watet begunchie/ ማርጭቄ/ ወተት፡ በጉንቼ፡፡/ Marchigie or Watet begunchie/ ማርጭቄ/ወተት፡ በጉንቼ/ is a type of Sorghum, very sweet when eaten. It seems that research has to be done about this plant. Ethiopia is unique in many things.

Belief

So far we were talking about the ecology of Ethiopia. Now let us also see the belief and other societal factors of this country. This country of the Horn is known as a cliché'in African studies. Since the belief of the people of Ethiopia has been Christianity for over one thousand six hundred years let us see in detail the Biblical aspects for a number of reasons.

1. Ethiopia is the 1st Christian country in Africa. King James Version mentions Ethiopia forty five times. In the continent of Africa the only country which believed in God Al Mighty based on the Bible since ancient times has been Ethiopia. Since the era of colonialism, however; thanks to missionaries Christianity is spreading in the continent of Africa at a rapid rate.
2. Ethiopia is the only country which was not colonized in the continent of Africa, except for a brief time by Italian Fascism after mid-1930.
3. Ethiopia is one of the most populous nations in Africa. The 1st is Nigeria.
4. Since 1963 Ethiopia headquarters African Unity (A.U.)

In ancient times the land of Ethiopian ancestors was called Punt. Later this part of Africa was called Abyssinian Empire. Today this part of the Horn of Africa is called Ethiopia.

Ethiopia is green all year round. However; due to recurrence of drought, it seems dry. But the cause of the drought is not nature. The cause of the drought is mismagement of the ecology of Ethiopia. So due to mismanagement and deforestation Ethiopia is becoming drier from time to time. In spite of these conditions Ethiopia has still many rivers and lakes. There is also abundant rainfall all year round in many places. For example look at Egypt and the Sudan which depends on the Nile whereby Egyptians and Sudanese lead a better life. In spite of the fertility of the soil, the reccurrence of rainfall and abundant rivers, lakes and streams, Ethiopia faces shortage of food. Though the cause is not clear them, people of the world are concerned about the starvation of Ethiopia all the time.

According to archaeologists early man emerged in Ethiopia about 3.5 million years ago. Evolution runs short of realiblity and credibility because archaeological information changes whenever their skilled scientists find new fossils and their findings are changing constantly.

Theory of Creation does not change its information and content. In the book of Creation every thing is realible and new. What God did for Stephen according to the Book of Acts, He will do it for you. He will let you to be stoned and go to heaven.

Ethiopia follows theory of Creation, whereas; though, archaeology believes in evolution, changes & circumstances. The Lord, however; whose principle is based on the 'Theory of Creation' does not change His mind according to circumstances and theory of Darwin. But Ethiopians in general for their life and destiny seems to follow and to embrace Wisdom, which is the other name of God. In the Book Habakkuk 3:6, it is written:
''Man's ways are changeable.
God's ways are everlasting.''

As mentioned above thanks Lord for allowing Ethiopia beginning from ancient times to believe in Him and to help them lead life according to His own designs and ways. Therefore; here after making this clear in our mind, we are going to see more illustrative explanations from the Bible and how Ethiopia believes in the Lord and gives her back to the changeable ways of man's philosophy.

Ethiopia in the Bible

When travellers want to visit an area, they need to know history of the country before they buy plane tickets. Knowledge of the country they want to visit helps them a lot in many ways. Knowledge is power. So as you travel in Ethiopia if some thing encites you about this ancient country open your Bible which is your source of wisdom, strength and history. So reading the following Chapters and verses will give you clues of the grain of truth about Ethiopia. The name of Queen Sheba is popular in history. I believe the history of Queen Sheba because Queen Sheba is mentioned in the Bible. So because the history of Queen Sheba is written in the Bible many believe that the history of the queen is true and not legendary. An individual with a legendary history does not at all appear in the Bible. The history of Queen Sheba has been distorted by authors who believe in legend. According to refrences given from the following chart you will learn the truth about about Jesus, Who is the Savior of your life.

* According to the Bible the book of Jeremiah Chapter 13:23 explains Ethiopia saying: '''Can the Ethiopian change his skin or the leopard his spots?'' Or ye also do well, that are accustomed to do evil?''
* According to the Bible the book of Psalm 68, Ethiopia shall soon stretch out her hands on to the Lord.
* According to the Bible the book of 1st Kings 10: 1 -13 explains that Queen Sheba, the Queen of Ethiopia in about 950 B.C. heared the fame of King Solomon concerning the name of the Lord and went to Jerusalem to celebrate God Al-Mighty.
* According to the Bible the book of Amos 9:7 God

said:"Israel, I am the Lord and the Ethiopians are no are no less important to me than you are."

* According to the Bible the book of Zephaniah 3:10 explains that from across the rivers of Ethiopia, My scattered people, My true worshippers, will bring offerings to Me.
* It is hardly possible to exhaust all what the Bible says about Ethiopia in this book. If you need more reading have glances at:-
* Genesis 2:13 explains that Gihon river / Abbay whose source is from the Garden of Eden emcompasses the whole of Ethiopia.
* In the Book of Numbers 12:1, Miriam and Aaron spoke against Moses because of the Ethiopian woman he married.
* The Book of Esther 1:1-9 talks about King Ahsuerus and he ruled from India to Ethiopia. Ester the Queen was his wife.
* According to the Book of Job 28:19 the Topaz of Ethiopia shall not equal wisdom; neither shall it be valued with pure gold. Job 28:18 is about the priceless value of wisdom. This verse tells us that all the topaz of Ethiopia and all the finest gold can not compare with it. See also Proverb 8:12 & 19. Therefore Topaz of Ethiopia might be the highest expensive gold. It is called timizimiz worq / ጥምዝምዝ ወርቅ/ in Amharic. Though topaz is a beautiful gold, wisdom is the best thing on earth.
* The Book of Isaiah 37:9 talks about Ethiopian king Tirhakah in the time Hezkiah, king of Judah.
* In the Book of Jeremiah 38:7-12 we learn that Ebene-Melech the Ethiopian takes Jeremiah the prophet out of the dungeon with rotten rags before he died.
* Jeremiah 46:1-10-says:" Let the mighty men, the Ethiopians and Lybians come forth and handle the shield, and the Lydians that handle and bend the bow."
* According to Book of Psalm 71(72):9 the Ethiopians shall bow before him and his enemies shall lick the dust.
* The Book of Acts 8:27-29 say:"... Behold a man of Ethiopia, and eunuch of great authority under Candace queen of the Ethiopians, who had the charge of all her

treasury, and had come to Jerusalem for to worship."
* According to 2nd Chronicles 8:18, -Queen Sheba heard the fame of King Solomon.

It is hardly possible to understand well or to write every thing what is in the Bible about Ethiopia. I have only written a little just for taste. So from among the above list, however; I have written in detail about the submission of the gentile Ethiopian queen to Al- Mighty Lord by 950 B.C. - Sources: 2nd Chronicles Chapter 8 verse 18, Author Belay Gidey

<u>Queen Sheba</u>

The history of Queen Sheba and King Solomon is one of the unique and interesting histories in the Bible. So many people are eager to know the history of Queen Sheba and King Solomon. Author Belay Gidey gives a detail historical account about ancient Ethiopian Civilization in his book:"የኢትዮጵያ ሥልጣኔ" According to Gidey, ancient Aksum was the capital of Queen Sheba. Even before 1000 B.C, long ago before the time of Queen Sheba, Ethiopia had kings and queens. According to Belay, Queen Sheba herself was the heir to the throne of her father Tewasia who was himself the 51st king of Ethiopia while his daughter Queen Sheba was the 52nd leader to come to the throne of Ethiopia.

226 kings from the Solomonic line and when Queen Sheba included 227 leaders ruled over Ethiopia for the last 3000 years. Out of these 227 kings and queens the best leaders of Ethiopia were Queen Sheba and Emperor Haile Selassie I for the following reasons.

In ancient times Ethiopia was a great nation. For example when Sheba came to power, Ethiopia was at the landmark /zenith of her power. Even in our age, during the reign of Emperor Haile Selassie I, the domain of Ethiopia extended from the northern tip of the present day Eritrea to the border of Moyale. In his Grand Era Emperor Haile Selassie tried to unite the whole of Africa. In his reign Ethiopia had also ports and huge ships that go to and fro the Red Sea and the Mediterranean world by and large.

In the time of Queen Sheba about 3000 years ago the power and domain of Ethiopia was large. This is because Queen Sheba ruled over a large area which extended from Egypt in the West, Yemen in the north, Tanzania in the east and Madagascar in the south.

In world history according to Belay Gidey Queen Sheba was kown as the Queen of the South.'' This was because she ruled over areas south of Israel and Yemen. When Ethiopia was at the zenith of her power she had trade relationship with Israel. Israel in those days was ruled by King Solomon, the wisest man on the surface of the earth. It was through her merchants especially through the head of the merchants whose name was Tamrin that Queen Sheba first heard about the Wisdom of Solomon.

Some times it is good to uncover the reality and reliability before every thing else and broadcast later about it. This is because some people who are not well informed about Ethiopian history consider that Queen Sheba was from Arabia. Still there are others who believe that there is a country known as Ethiopia somewhere in Asia.

When one hears such type of things repeatedly from intellectuals it is confusing, and it is hardly possible which one to believe. Every thing has to be told according to evidence.

There is no tangible evidence that Queen Sheba was from Arabia. The confusion might be created due to the fact that Ethiopia in the time of the Queen, Ethiopia under the leadership of Queen Sheba was rulling over a very large area making her capital at Axum and expanding from Axum as far as Yemen. This might be beyond expectation for some when they see these days down – sized, economically poor and politically weak Ethiopia at this time. But what should be taken into account is that; even though, Ethiopia is weak and poor her history does not change by present circumstances. This must be clear, because in ancient times, in the near past or in the present time, there is no any other country by the name Ethiopia in any part of Asia and no queen by the name Queen Sheba in any other part of the world, except Queen Sheba, the queen of Ethiopia and the biblically well documented Queen Makeda. In the time of Queen Sheba/ Queen Makeda, Aksum was well known for her trade with the Meditranean world, for minting coins, constructing tall monuments/ stelae and for possessing the Ark of the Covenant.

Light is the symbol of Jesus. Darkness is the symbol of the evil spirit. It is always wonderful if light twinkles and darkness glooms. This is because light is better than darkness. In Spiritual affairs of course when we say light, we are talking about the spread of the teachings of Jesus. In the Scriptures we know that Jesus is the symbol of light. Of course Jesus is not only the symbol of light, we know that Himself is the light and life of mankind. Ethiopia knew about Jesus or AlMighty Lord or the Morning Star when He twinkled in her life by 950 B.C., and that was in the time of Queen Sheba. This is what Belay Gidey tried to address in his book.

Once people know about God Al-Mighty they have no problem of knowing their way. When there is light, there is no problem of knowing the way. Adversely, however; it is when one feels darkness he has a problem of knowing his way. For example take the history of Ethiopia. Since early 1970's Ethiopia does not know her way because of her rejection of the light of the worldand embracing the aetheist communist government, the symbol of darkness. To stretch her hands and to shout slogans that glorify darkness was her problem under communism.

To turn back to God and to read the Bible is a marvelous thing. There is no wrong in doing this. Take for example Thomas, one of the deciples of Jesus. When Thomas asked Jesus, " How can we know the way?" Jesus told Thomas that He is the way, the truth and life." See John 14:5-6. This is also the question of many people. To know the way, the truth and life you better know Jesus first and to know Jesus read the Bible, pray and fast. Ask Him to reveal Himself to you.

So as mentioned above, ever since Ethiopia heard about God Al-Mighty she has been walking in light. Even when Communism infiltrated in 1970's to destroy her light, the fire was glowing and spreading.

Now many who emerged in the time of Communist Ethiopia spread the word of God through out the world. How marvelous it is. When communism died, they are alive. With out fear under in the era of Communism the young generation was reading the Bible and it was hardly possible for Communists to prevent the spread of the Gospel and believers from dancing and worshipping the Lord.

History repeats itself from time to time. According to Genesis 1:1-4 when God commanded light to shine, darkness was lost. So as time passed by while Communism symbol of darkness crumbles evangelism which is symbol of light shines brighter than ever before.

Because light is good, it is God's will to separate light from dark according to Genesis 1:3. It is also God's will to shine His light over elsewhere. People of Ethiopia are also eager to get more of the bright light of God these days because they know that when man knows about God, he does not want to walk with out Him. Every thing with out Him is dark. (John8:12) Every thing with out Jesus is prison. With Jesus every thing is cute and heaven.

Queen Sheba was a gentile queen. At first this cute queen was a queen with out true God. But she sought to know the true God. God revealed for her when she was eager to know Him. When God revealed to her, she opened the door of belief, holding light in her hands for the rest of her people. So it becomes the will of God to make her whole reign peaceful and to write her name in the Book of life, the Bible. In the same token if leaders also open their hearts to Jesus, they will rule for long time with peace and dignity. This is tested in time and in the laboratory of Axumite palace. This was tested 3000 years ago. This is because the idea of knowing the true God was introduced into Ethiopia through Queen Sheba in 950 B.C. After that not only Ethiopians have known about God, but also they have known how to worship Lord Al-Mighty Himself.

Today is no different from yesterday. The Word of God is same all the time. Since the Word of God is not fiction, it does not change. It is real all the time. It is life.This book gives its witness, because God is real. He is not only a real person but also a

Savior. God the Savior and the Creator saves us from wrath and corruption, giving us us a new heart and giving us birth for the second time.

The Creative power of God never ends. He looks at the heart of man constantly. He always wants man to have a new heart. He asks man to have a new heart so that he could be wise. After becoming wise through the will of God, he is no more a foolish person. He says yes for any thing God says. For example when God asks him to be born again, he says 'yes.'

Are you a wise person? Do you have common sense to understand this? It is not nuclear physics. It is simple to understand. Do you like to be born again like Nichodemus? If you are born again accepting Jesus you will be saved from the wrath of the Lord. Once you are saved your family according to the Bible will be saved too.

To be a Christian is great. To become Christian is wisdom and wisdom gives light pushing aside the dark. The greatest day for a man is the time that he becomes Christian or the time God installs light in his body. It is unbelievable how early in the history of man kind in general and in the history of Africa in particular God gives wisdom and light wrapped together to Ethiopia.

Package of Wisdom and light is found in the Gospel. Ethiopia is one of the early nations which received the Gospel. It is unbelievable how the Lord has brought Ethiopia with bright life that still shines to these days and also how He still preserves her light in these last days when news of ungodly character of people in the world is spreading far and wide. It is also pity when many countries accept Jesus at a fast rate, Christianity is growing at a slow pace these days in Ethiopia though it is also a ''Good News'' to hear that other countries of Africa are giving glory to Jesus accepting and believing in Him.

To know a little bit about how people of Ethiopia worship the Lord, let us start from the Ark of Covenant. The Ark, the holy ultimate of reality of faith and worship, helps Ethiopia to be recognized as a unique place in biblical history. Of course among the Israelites, in ancient times, the Ark was known as a sincere place of worship and prayer and because Ethiopia followed the trend of the Israelites, she too has become a sincere place to worship the Lord. This is not an exaggeration. If one wants to see how Ethiopians worship the Lord, he can check one of the Ethiopian Churches around him. I have also heard from people outside Ethiopia when they say that Ethiopians have a zeal for the Lord. This type of explanation might seem strange for the reader of this book. But there is no any other explanation beyond the history and the reality. But the people of Ethiopia comprehending that the Ark is precursor of Jesus are now seeking Salvation as mentioned herewith.

According to Ephesians 2:14, Christ brought Jews and Gentiles together by'' breaking the wall of hatred, '' that separated them. This happened after Christ died on the Cross to liberate mankind according to Ephesians 1:7 and 8. It is wrong to stop here. It is necessary to mention His resurrection. This is because after His resurrection or better to say, after God has raised Him from death and has let sit Him at God's right side in heaven according to Ephesians 1:20. But long before Jesus's resurrection, in the Old Testament, Israel and Ethiopia were united in belief. They believed the same Jehovah or God Father.

Paul was the chosen instrument to bring the message of God to the Gentiles. But prior to Paul, Ethiopia was the only gentile country that had strong attachment and faith with Al-Mighty Lord through the people of Israel. Down here is the story of how this was possible.

It is a real fact that long time has passed before Paul was chosen to tell the gentiles about the Al-Mighty Lord. In those days, God's hand was on Ethiopia. Also in those days people of Israel in the Old Testament were in the Period of the Exodus. Period of Exodus might have started in the time of Moses according to B.W. Anderson in about 1300 B.C. Alittle later Ethiopia in the time of Queen Sheba in about 950 B.C. had made strong relationship with people of Israel. It was probably at that time that Ethiopia believed in the God of Israel. This portrays that it was over 950 years later after Ethiopia was fully aware of the lordship of the Mighty God that Apostle Paul started teaching about the " Good News", to the gentiles. This shows that since long time ago God's plan for Ethiopia is 'hope and success and not suffering.' - (Jeremiah 29:11)

God's plan for Ethiopia is mysterious. Here is the story. As every one knows Israelites are the chosen people in the world. Also according to God's promise Israel was/is the first country that was/ is able to get God's glorious transformation from humanity's fallen nature into the divine life. We say that Israel was/ is the first country to get God's glorious transformation from mankind's fallen nature into divine nature because Jesus was not only born in Israel, but also it is in this part of the Israelite world He revealed heavenly secretes to humanity. In fact the world by and large has got blessings from Israel. Take for example the Bible and all the authors of the Bible are all from Israel, and one of the few gentile countries of the world which has been the heir to the showers of blessings of Israel since time of immemorial is Ethiopia and this is the point that this book wants to tackle.

We have seen above how Ethiopia to our surprise had become partaker of God's promise long time before the birth of Christ. This country known as the "Horn of Africa " became partaker and / or heir of God's promise through Queen Sheba at first and then through the Ark of Covenant beginning from about 950 B.C. Some people might think today that Ethiopia just holds the Ark of Covenant and does not believe in Jesus. By the way Jesus is not 2000 years old. He is the Alpha and Omega. In fact it was Ethiopia which knew about Jesus early in the history of mankind far earlier or before 2000 years. Early Ethiopians were aware that the Ark of Covenant is the precursor of Jesus and this proves that Ethiopia is all timer believer of Jesus.

Though Ethiopians had the Ark of Covent long time before Jesus when they heard about His birth they started a new Calendar, the Ethiopian Calendar to show their acceptance of Him and to glorify His mercy and it is the birth of Jesus which initiated early Ethiopians start the Ethiopian calander, which is popularly is known as the "Year of Mercy." Today people of Ethiopia believe in Jehovah / God the Father/ Jesus / the Son of God, and in the Holy Spirit.

God has hot relationship with people of Israel beginning from Abraham, the patriarch and then through the consecutive generations that descended down to Isaac, Jacob and others. A person who believes that Abraham is the father of Israel is wise, because he believes in'' Abraham as his grand father.'' In the Old Testament, Ethiopia believed that God of Israel, God of Abraham and God of Isaac was also her God. This is good because she believes in a righteous father from the very beginning.

To believe in ''Abraham as a father'' is a good thing. There are lots of shower of blessings in believing in''Abraham as a father.'' I am talking about the real original Abraham. There are also people who create ''their own Abraham as a father'' in order to get help through him. Such people are those who make strong relationship with an important person in order to get support through him. Take for example getting a good job through him. Pending this for a while let us continue with Ethiopia.

A wise person always takes the best. Ethiopia is wise because she takes the best in the history of mankind. . In the New Testament, when Jesus Christ is manifested fully in humanity (Colossians 1:19) Ethiopia accepted Jesus Christ as her Savior. When Ethiopia accepted Jesus, she dwells in Jesus and Jesus dwells in the heart of Ethiopians. Then after that Ethiopia started to declare that Jesus is the Savior of mankind. People of Ethiopia call Jesus, Medihane Alem/ መድኃኔ፡ አለም/ meaning the Savior of the world. The years after the birth of Jesus are also called Amete Mihiret/አመተ፡ ምሕረት/ - meaning 'Years of Mercy.' Man is sinner, but through the mercy of God he has hope to go to paradise/ or heaven and this is the time of mercy, the hope to go to heaven. Thanks to Jesus for He has paid the price.

When I was a young boy in Ethiopia I was able to read and write. In those days nobody was able to read or write in my neighbourhood. They were not educated. So they ask me to read letters that they received from far off relatives and friends. When I read the letters towards the end I used to read a statement which says: 'if God of Israel wills, 'we will see each other eye to eye and face to face. In those days I started to notice that Ethiopia believes the same true God like the Israelites since ancient times. I started to believe that God of Israel is God of Ethiopia. That was Old Testament belief. In the New Testament Ethiopia is able to become heir of the body of Christ and partaker of God's promise in Christ through the Gospel. (Eph 3:6)

We have seen above how the attachment of Ethiopia with God Al-Mighty lasted for a long time. So because of her long attachment and love for Christ, Christianity in Ethiopia has a long history. Really Ethiopians love Christ. They fail short to express their love for God. So because they have the zeal for Jesus, they bow down and kneel in prayer just as Paul has done to express his love for Al-Mighty Lord. (See-Ephesians 3:14)

The mission of Ethiopians is to open their mouths to glorify the Lord. Whenever they want to spread the 'Good News,' they shout loud '' Elil! Elil!/ ዕልል... ዕልል:: Shouting loud they express their joy in the Lord and their belief in Him. They did this thinking, enjoying and believing that God loves and enjoys such things. It is good if every body works according to his gift and ability. What is needed is to do every thing for the glory of God.

In the 1st century A.D. the well known evangelist was Paul. Apostle Paul was a great man of God. He was the one known for spreading the Word of God to different people of the world. He was the one to write most of the New Testament books. He was lso known for his teaching, preaching and planting Churches. In one way or another, the Gospel is spreading like wild fire in a forest. Nonethelss; Apostle Paul is highly accredited as the well evangelist in the history of mankind for spreading and telling us the 'Good News' according Romans 1:1.

Ethiopians don't only bow down from their head and heart they also kneel from their knees and open their mouths with joy to pray and to praise the Lord shouting and calling the name of the Supreme Lord, Jesus Christ!/ ኢየሱስ ክርስቶስ/ Long time ago when I was very young, I remember when the rain was late members of our community used to go out in the open air, and altogether in agreement praying for the rain to come. I also remember towards the end of their prayer they used to agree to shout on to the Lord looking towards the atmosphere. When they shout they used to say: Oh! Lord, Mercy Lord. We need rain for our farm. In Amharic this means:"ኦ! ዕግዚኦ! ኦ!ኦ! መሀረነ:ክርስቶስ:: "ኦ! ዕግዚኦ! ኦ!: መሀረነ:ክርስቶስ::" "ኦ! ዕግዚኦ! መሀረነ: ክርስቶስ::"

Asking the mercy of God is indeed a great thing. This helps God to allow and to send shower of blessings for His people. This is because God says:" I promise that when any two of you on earth agree about something, you are praying for, my father in Heaven will do it for you. ''Whenever two or three of you come together in my name, I am there with you. '' Source: Matthew 18:19-20. In the same way, just like our forefathers if now the people of different villages in Ethiopia pray in agreement ask God what they want, He will do it for the sake of His name and for the sake of His word.

Before the arrival of the Ark of Covenant, there was darkness in Ethiopia. But when the light came from Jerusalem glittering and accompanied by the Ten Commandments, the old idols, which were tags of unbelief crumbled down. Ethiopia accepted the Ten Commandments. The commandments of God differed from the moral codes of the ancient religion. The Jews came to Ethiopia by 950 B.C. accompanying the Ark of Covenant. Together with Ark and the Jews, the Jewish tradition legacy of the Ten Commandments of the Lord arrived in Ethiopia. If you go to Ethiopia today you will see Jewish tradition in Gondar, Wollo, Gojjam, and Tigray and in many parts of the region which was formerly called Abyssinia.

The Ten Commandments in the Old Testament show God's awesome majesty. The resurrection of Jesus in the New Testament shows the boundless mercy, goodness, grace and the lordship of Al-Mighty in the whole universe. Again this shows that Ethiopia knew God's awesome, boundless goodness, God's grace, mercy, and the only true God, the Alpha and Omega since at least in 950 B.C.

Many times people's history and biography looks good. But the history of such people often bubbles and withers away leaving behind nothing worthy. The history of Queen Sheba is quite different from this type of history. The history of Apostle Paul is different from this type of history. The history of the disciples of Jesus is different from such type of biography because all these people mentioned died in faith. With out faith according to Hebrews 11:6 no one pleases God. Faith always speaks even after one dies according to Hebrews 11:4. For no reason this book mentions the names of these people because as the Bible says God Himself is happy with these people. For reference - See Hebrews Chapter 11, to study the great faith of God's people.

Queen Sheba had a great Empire and many palaces. When she lived on earth, every thing was nothing for her. But she was finding a better way to reserve a home in the heaven according to Hebrews 11:15-16. .

Unless one is happy he can not enjoy. Even if one enjoys life for some time that joy lasts only for a brief period if it is only from the flesh. But when the joy is from AlMighty God, it is endless. So since the arrival of the Ark of Covenant in Ethiopia and since the birth of Jesus, the joy of Ethiopians has always grown from time to time; though; the decreases since 1970's and that were due to aetheist influence.

Since 4th century A.D in Timket, time of Baptism, Ethiopia's joy has always been high. Whether one was rich or poor or no matter what type of burden everyone faced in life, everybody was always happy and hungry for the abiding presence of God.

In a vast country like Ethiopia it is hardly possible to speak in general terms. There are people who philosophize and depend on their own philosophy. There are people with different religions. There are all sorts of people and it is hardly possible to generalize. But it is possible to talk about the people who lived in Ethiopia since time of immemorial accepting the legacy of their forefathers and heritage of Christianity. So in this case ever since the arrival of the Ark of Covenant, people of Ethiopian origin who believe in the Ark of the Covenant are filled with great pleasure, because these people whenever they see the Ark, the sacred object of the Lord are filled with joy and so they say:" Elil....Elil ..../ ዕሴል... ዕሴል.../

Therefore believing God in their midst, enthroned

in the Ark and carried by high priests in front of them, Ethiopians feel the maximum joy that words, phrases and statements can not express. So whenever they see the Ark they shout over and over again for words, phrases and statements cannot express their joy, they simply shout saying:"Elil!.. Elil!.. Elil!.. Elil!.." ./ ዕልል... ዕልል.../.. - This is Ethiopian way of expression of joy.

The momentum of their pleasure from the pit of their stomach increases and as they shout "Esey!..Esey!..Esey!..." ዕሰይ! ዕሰይ! Elil!.. Elil!.. ./ ዕልል... ዕልል.../.. Esey! Esey!. !." ዕሰይ! ዕሰይ! Esey! !..." ዕሰይ! Elil!..Elil!."

Queen Sheba who was amazed at Solomon's wisdom was breathless when she saw his palace, servants and their food arrangement, his officials, the sacrifices he offered at the Lord's Temple. (See -1st Kings Chapter 10.)

We recall our memory; the Ark of Covenant was in the Lord's Temple after Solomon built the temple according to the divine order. Therefore when Queen Sheba saw the Ark of Covenant whereby the Lord is invisibly enthroned, she was breathless. So she said to Solomon:-"I praise the Lord, your God. He is pleased with you and has made you king of Israel. The Lord loves Israel, so He has given them a king who will rule fairly and honestly." 1st Kings 10:9

The Ark

The history of the Ark of Covenant is found in the Bible if you open in the Book of Exodus Chapter 25. According to the Book of Exodus, the Ark is sacred thing of God because it contains the Ten Commandments. It was also built by the will and instruction of God Al-Mighty Himself. When God planned to construct the Ark, He had a plan to rest Himself in the Ark and to do wonders and miracles in the midst of the population. So according to His plan, when people of Israel carried the Ark and moved with Ark unexpected miracles were done. Take for example what happened on Joshua 3:15-16. Jordan River was separated to open the way for the people of Israel. Take another example, the story of the wall of Jericho. That is the wall of Jericho crumbled when when people of Israel moved around the city of Jericho seven times and shouted carrying the Ark. (See – Joshua 6:4-20). So because of this, the people of Israel carrying the Ark of Covenant moved from place to place enjoying the miracle of God.

Movement of the Ark in Israel

Ever since the time of its construction in Sinai, the Ark of Covenant was used by the Israelites in different battlefields to gain successive victories. The longest time that the Ark rested was in Shiloh, the ancient shrine. When Ark was in Shiloh, the people of Israel sinned and failed to give due glory and honor to the Lord. So to the shock of every one, especially to the priests and to the guilty behavior of everyone, the Ark favoured wilderness than residing in Shiloh. So according to the 1st Samuel 4:11 the Ark moved from Shiloh to the Phillipines when the Phillipines captured the Ark. Again according to 1st amChapter 6 the Phillipines sent back the Ark to the people of Israel. The Ark then stayed in Abinadab's house, his son, Elezar taking care of it for three months according to 1st Sam Chapter 7.

When the Ark moved from Mount Zion or the city of David to the temple of the Lord in Jerusalem there was no more wandering it just settled down. The Ark of course settled down in Jerusalem until it moved out of Israel and left for Ethiopia and settled down in Aksum since then.

Let us say a few things, at this juncture about God's visitation of Israel. It seems that when God wants to visit a country, He gives a good leader. When God gives Israel, Solomon as the king, it was a great visitation, because Solomon was a brilliant leader, blessed with in sight and understanding. He was wiser in all of Judah and in all of Israel and even in the whole world than anybody else. He was a wise person that could talk wisely about anything, be it plants, animals reptiles and even fishes. (1st Kings 4:29-34)

Now let us go back to the point where we were

talking about the permanent residence of the Ark of Covenant in Solomon's Temple. God is not like every one of us. He is marvelous. Once He says, He says it! He does not want to change His decision looking around circumstances.

However, when the Lord wants to make a covenant or a promise, He wants His people to give Him the honor that is accrued to Him. So when they sin He wants people to pray and turn back. After that He just forgives them. But if they don't turn back choosing other gods, He will abandon them. So He had told Israelites from the very beginning that He would leave them if they start worshipping other gods. So from the very beginning He had told them to be aware of what He is doing, saying, "This temple is now magnificent. But if you desert Me, I will desert the Temple where I said I would be worshipped. When thee things happen, every one who walks by it will be shocked and will ask, "Why did the Lord do such a terrible thing to His people and to this temple? (2nd Chronicles 7:12- 21)

In life we cannot double-cross friends and expect them to stay with us. Every time God proves Himself the best friend of mankind. He is well known for staying with us. So it is not good to depart on our behalf as well. It is not good to put anything in His place. It is said that Solomon married an Egyptian princess by the name Makshara. She was well noted for her beliefs of idols and for seducing Solomon to agree and to make the temple of God a worshiping place for idols. It is said that he loves Makshara very much. On the other hand when Solomon's love for God decreased or wanted, his wisdom decreased. The Lord is a tough judge. Thus Solomon devoting himself to women during the last part of his eleven years of his life, he died at sixty years of his age.
(E.W.Budge – The Queen of Sheba and her only son Menelik – 1922 printed by Medici Society Limited, London. Page is found in the introductory part and that is IXXX.)

Journey of the Ark from Jerusalem to Ethiopia

When I remember a dream, I am aware of a number of things. In the first place I learn to remember my dreams. I should not forget dreams that I saw in my life. We should not forget our dreams. I also believe that King Solomon the wisest person on earth might not have forgotten his dream that he saw even after twenty-two years he had his way with Queen Sheba. The dream he saw, was:" A brilliant sun coming down from heaven, greatly shinning over Israel and then withdraws to Ethiopia." The Amharic translation of this dream is:" ከንግስቲትዋ ፡ጋር ፡ተኝቶ፡ ሳለ፡ ንጉስ፡ ሰሎሞን፡ ጸሀይ፡ ከዕስራኤል ፡ ምድር፡ ላይ፡ ዝቅ፡ ብላ ፡ዕስክ ፡ኢትዮጵያ፡ ድረስ ፡ስትአበራ ፡ምድሩንም፡ በብርሀንዋ ፡ስትአነጻብርቅ ፡በህልሙ ፡ ተመለከተ፡፡

In terms of time zone Ethiopia and Israel are the same. This is because they are in the same longitude. The Movement of the Ark from Jerusalem to Ethiopia was directly south wards. So the sun gives light from geographycal point of view for both Ethiopia and I srael at the same time. But King Solomon saw in dream Ethiopia getting brighter light than that of Israel.

In the context of the story, can you guess what Solomon saw in dream was about the loss of the Ark. According to history the Ark of the Covenant was the light of Israel. Because God was allowing the Ark of Covenant to stay in Ethiopia, He told Solomon in his dream that the Ark/ the light of Israel / was going out of Israel to Ethiopia and was dwelling in Ethiopia. Spiritually this was why the light in Ethiopia was brighter than that of Israel.

Ethiopia is in North-East Africa. Israel is in South-West Asia. So the Ark moved directly south wards from Israel to Ethiopia. The Jews who accompanied Menelik, son of King Solomon and Queen Sheba carrying the Ark moved fast with out looking to the left or to the right. In Ethiopia, the Ark arrived at first in Lake Tana near Axum, the place where Queen Sheba was ruling and residing at her beautiful palaces.

The movement of the Ark was fast because the Ark and the team that accompanied Menilik were filled by the Spirit of the Lord and according to legendary sources heavenly chariots were carrying the team so that the group could reach Ethiopia with in a short time.

The Ark first moved from Jerusalem to Lake Tana. After the Ark reached Ethiopia, it had also moved from place to place with in Ethiopia. So after arriving in Lake Tana it moved to Aksum. From Axum it moved to Lake Zewai according to Gram Hancock, the author of the Book, the Sign and the Seal. Finally it moved back to Axum.

The sketch map of the Movement of the Ark From Jerusalem to Ethiopia

There are many stories, which tell how the Ark of Covenant came to Ethiopia. As to the direction there is no other way than travelling sout directly. So there is no other way to imagine. Some Israelites might suspect Solomon had allowed his son to take it away to Ethiopia. This has no grain of truth. For such people this must be clear. Solomon did not arrange such a thing to happen. He just only saw a dream. The Ark was taken away with out Solomon's knowledge and with out his permission says E.W. Budge, the author of Queen Sheba and her only son Menelik. That is certain, as I have stated in another place that the Ark was stolen.

The Ark which was lost was the one which was constructed by Moses supported by Oholiab who was also ordered by God from the Dan tribe given the wisdom, and also Bezalel, a craftsman from the Judah tribe.Source- Exodus 31:1-5) Therefore this was the original Ark which we are talking about and that which was stolen- Source – Ahistory of Ethiopia by Harold Marcus- page 8.) There are also many stories, which explain how the Ark of Covenant was lot or how it came to Ethiopia.

The holy cargo left Jerusalem carrying the Ark of Covenant escorted by a number of Israeli nobles crossed the Red Sea, heading southwards to Ethiopia. After Menelik and his escortees crossed the Red Sea, they advanced to Ethiopia as many of the oral informants narrate in Ethiopia following the banks of the Rivers of Nile, Atbara, and Tekeze and finally rested in Lake Tana. One may ask a question saying: "How did the Israelites discover that whether the Ark is lost of not?

Behold, it comes to pass that one time in the morning when the schedule for worshipping the Lord arrived, the children of Israel and the priests went into the house of God to pray. Behold again! It came to pass that, when the priests ended glorifying the Lord, kneeling in supplications and falling prostrate, worshipping the Monarch of the universe, the Ark did not rise up into the air, and it did not stir from its place. There was no holy Spirit in the service:- See:/ E.W. Budge and the Civilization of Ethiopia -የኢትዮጵያ ሥልጣኔ / by Belay Gidey page 14-15.

The Spirit of the Lord works all the time. God does not rest. Especially in Church service and when an individual prays the work of Holy Spirit is high. When Holy Spirit is high there is miracle. So this shows that there is a difference between the Lord and other idols. When there is no Holy Spirit there is no joy or miracle. People who serve idols have no joy or miracles at all.

Contrary to passive idols Our Lord is always active. He has no break or day off to pour his joy upon His people. He is also always miraculous and victorious. He is always creating new things. People who have faith in Him are also victorious because they also see miracles when they work in His Mighty Name, Jesus Christ. (Source – E.W. Budge)

In the case of the Temple of Solomon in the time when the Ark was lost when the Lord did not react, the priests said, behold! "Some one has sinned; we should fast and pray for three days to search the person that sinned." After saying that, they fasted and prayed for three days. They could not find the person that committed sin. Thereafter, there followed, oh! After that a lot of terror, fear and calamity among the priests happened.

When they could not find a guilty person or folks that sinned, the priests went up the Tabernacle, where the Ark of Covenant rested and searched for the Ark itself. To their excitement they found an empty case, resting upon the place where the Tabernacle had stood. They knew after that for certain that the son of King Solomon, Menelik had taken it away. This time, the priests and elders of Israel went to King Solomon weeping, to tell him about the absence of the Ark of Covenant from its holy shrine. This time King Solomon wept and cried out in pain. He showed exceedingly great sorrow. Oh! On that day the heart of all people felt with grief, and King Solomon himself showing exceedingly great sorrow than everybody else remained helpless.

Israeli priests and elders seeing Solomon feeling pity and hopeless started to comfort him saying: "May the king live!" They also uggested to him to dispatch an armed force to pursue his son and his escort, and take from him the holy Covenant of God, and to bring it back to "His Sacred House". Solomon as requested gave those soldiers, money and provisions. The group set out following the young man. They rode on their way for forty days. – (Source- E.W. Budge)

Now hold on please. Hold on gives time to think. Someone has a question. Was the group aware that they were following the Ark of Covenant? Were they pretty sure that the Ark of Covenant had its own will? Was the group that accompanied Menilik sure that the Ark could make miracles? If we go back and examine the history why it was constructed we would certainly understand why it was constructed, and we would certainly recall what it did in the time of Israel's wilderness.

Actually the Ark was made to the privilege of the people of Israel to help them in their journey of wilderness. But if we remember the dream of Solomon we will come to our mind. So what do we notice when we see the Ark of Covenant was running away from the people of Israel? And what do we think when we remember the clue word which shows the fulfillment of the dream? So what do you think when the clue word pinpoints the dream that dealt with: "The sun withdrew, and it never turned back."

Now again let us go back to our narration of the journey of the Ark towards Ethiopia and to the group running after Menelik and his escort. While the group followed Menelik and his escort at a great speed they found merchants riding back towards their home. They asked those merchants if they had seen a group advancing forward. The merchants stopped for a while to tell information to the group. Then they told them that they had seen a tabernacle, a great king, numbers soldiers, and in doubt talked about the box of the Covenant of God, and how they travelled saying:" ... were travelling along like the clouds, driven by Mighty Winds for long distances at a time." They also told them what the natives along which the group passed by told them saying:" natives of the villages through which they have passed informed them that Menilik's group traveled each day the distance of forty days' journey."

When the group dispatched by Solomon following Menelik's escort, they got reliable news from merchants that the escortees were travelling very fast to Ethiopia. This time Solomon's messangers were desperate and disheartened, and decided to return home to Isreal. (Source- E.W.Budge) Pending this for a while let us see the Lord's purpose for Ethiopia.

The Lord has a purpose for Ethiopia, "His chosen people." He gave up Himself to Ethiopia travelling in the form of Mighty winds and leading Menilik and His group. This is not the end of the story.

Once the Ark of Covenant reached safe in Ethiopia and after it first resided in Lake Tana and spent most its life in Aksum it was also travelling in different parts of Ethiopia for safety purposes.

Since the Ark resided in Ethiopia, people did not question about it. They just accepted it and revered it. It seemed that God had opened their spiritual eyes. This might be because it was due to the presence of God that people of Ethiopia placed a strong devotion on the Ark. They just started to express their Ethiopian excited way of expression of joy. By the way joy does not come by itself. It is given from God. The Ethiopian way of expression of joy especially common among the female section of the population is to say:"Elil! Elil!"- ዕልል: ዕልል

It is surprising how people of Ethiopia understood how mighty the Lord is. Such type of belief with out seeing or watching the miracles of God is a marvelous thing. This might be the reason why the Lord says: "my chosen people," Nobody knows these people. But God knows them. Especially those who strongly believe in the Son,-(Ethiopian word Wold) Jesus Christ have got reservation in heaven for such people. They don't have money, but they have heaven. They just praise the Lord. Praising is the fruit of the mouth. Praising the Lord is the sweet smell and savor for the Lord. Ethiopians are obsessed of praising the Lord. It is their joy. The Amharic word is elilita. When saying elil! They are very much happy, faint and breathless. They enjoy the love of the Lord. But watch out God does not look people en mass. He watches individuals. So every individual should accept Jesus as His Savior and that is the master key to go to heaven.

Though, it is physically portable wooden box, the Tabot which is like the original Ark of covenant, is placed in the innermost of the holy of holies of the Church. Every Ark made in Ethiopia is same with original Jewish architectural style. Also until Communist infiltration into Ethiopia, Ethio- Jewish relationship was a good one. Though; the plan of God for Ethiopia was wonderful, Communist shuffled slowly into Ethiopia to steal her independence propagating using rosy words. Of course to mislead

the people of Ethiopia when Communists annexed Ethiopia through their puppets they came shouting fake slogan of equality. One of the fake slogans of Communists was: "ዕኣል: በይ: አገሪ:
Meaning: Let my country enjoy
You are a nation of equality.

Politics is a dirty game. It looks wonderful when you hear about it. But be aware of its hidden motives. Check it 1st. See it from behind. Seen from behind it is dirty. Take care of politics. It is like a thief that comes to steal and destroy. When Communism entered into Ethiopia, their propagandists 1st studied the tradition of Ethiopia. They knew that the people of Ethiopia like to shout to express their joy, saying: " ዕልል: ዕልል:" So they came to destroy Ethiopia shouting the Ethiopian tradition of joy- namely: " ዕልል: ዕልል:" " ዕልል: ዕልል:" (ዕልል: በሉ·) This is what politics looks like. Propagation led Ethiopia to Soviet Russia's robbery. Nonetheless people of Ethiopia did not waste time to understand what was going on. Shortly after its establishment, people understood what socialism is all about and started to say Ah! Socialism! They regretted. It was too late. From time to time people's joy was changing to sadness. – It changed from joy to sadness. Every one regretted

Now let us go back to what is pending. Ethiopia of course has got a Tabot in every parish or wherever a Church is built. However; the real Ark of Covenant is found in Aksum Tsion. Whenever the Tabot comes out from the holy of holies or kiduse kidusan lots of people praise the Lord with joy. This is done occasionally and on special holidays like Epiphany or Timket. When the Tabot comes out of the holy of holies, it is surrounded by a large crowd of people, and usually this large crowd does not get closer to the Ark but instead they wait a few yards away from the Ark.

The Ark of covenant called in Ethiopia Tabot or Ark of Zion, is the center of devotion, worship, gift offering and center of sacrifice for the Lord. The strongest joy of the people of Ethiopia during Church service is to worship the Lord as the Ark comes out from the holy of holies. The heart of Ethiopians is open for the Lord. But most people do not have the Bible. The missionaries over there are also few. So to fill the vacuum more teachers and teaching materials and radio and TV stations like TBN are not working over there. If more missionaries go over there more souls would be saved when they teach that the Ark of Covenant is the precursor of Jesus. Here one could foresee one thing. The need for more evangelists has to be clear for missionaries of the world by and large to Ethiopia. So for the fulfillment of this it good to pray to the God of the heavens according to Nehemia 2:4 for blessing, reconstruction and visitation of the people of Ethiopia by the Lord to be accomplished to its fullest extent. For that matter history helps to study the past and to foresee the future and this is why the history of the Ark of Covenant is written in this book.

The Ark in Ethiopia

Since the arrival of the Ark of Covenant in Ethiopia, the Ark is called Tabot or the Ark of Zion in Amharic. In Ethiopia, the Ark of Zion is the center of devotion and worship. People of Ethiopia when they devote themselves to God they are filled with joy. Even when they hear about the name God/ Jesus/ or the Ark they are filled with joy. They utter calling the name of the Lord, saying repeatedly. "God of Israel" የõሥራ·ኤል አምላክ.

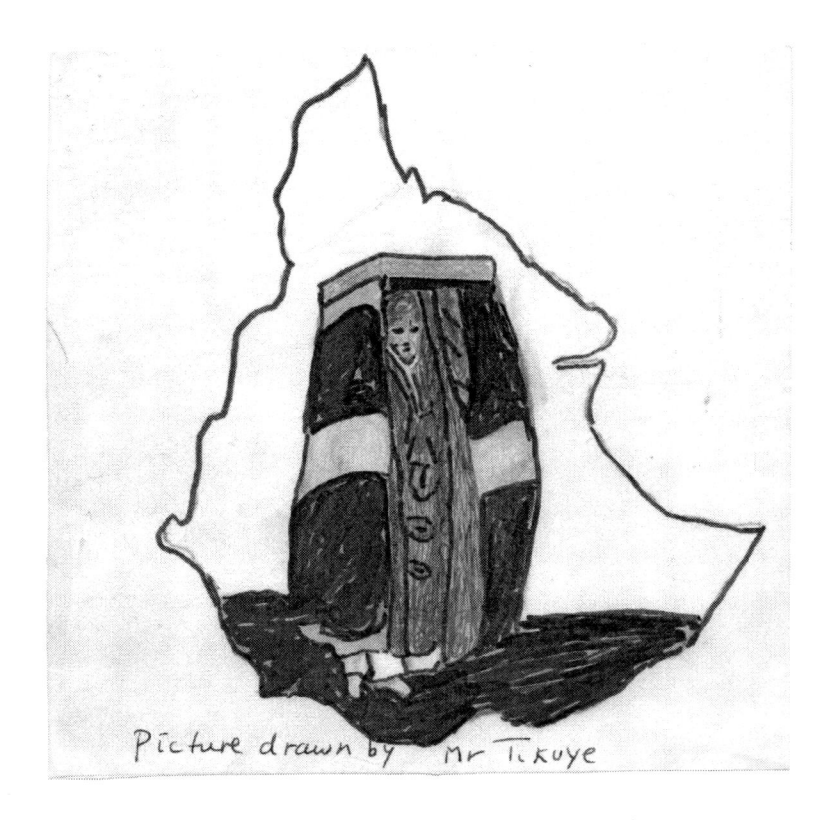

A priest carrying the Ark in Ethiopia

We learn a lot from this ancient country of Ethiopia a nation noted for her distinct history and varied culture, which dates back to ancient times. The distinct culture and varied culture of Ethiopia was clear to the out side world since the Axumite civilization and since the Ethiopian Empire was known as the Aksumite kingdom.

The Kingdom of Aksum extended in the north to Arabia. Aksumite Kingdom was a great power along with Persia China and Rome. Large amount of coins was minted and issued in Aksum. The minting of coins helped Aksum to facilitate her trade relations with India and China. Great edifices and dams were erected in Aksum and scientific and philosophical works were translated into Geez, one of the earliest written languages. Christianity became the state religion of the Aksumite Kingdom in 330 A.D. The Orthodox Church represents the oldest unbroken Christian Church in the Aksumite Empire. It was also in Aksumite Empire that the Ethiopian Jews, Bete Israel or Falasha, whose history goes back to King Solomon and the first Temple, lived. The very first Moslems, fleeing persecution in Mecca also sought and got refuge in the Aksumite Kingdom.

The history of Church in Ethiopia is part of the history of Tabot or the Ark of the Covenant. A Tabot is a tablet, which is called Tsilat. A Tsilat is on which the Geez version of the Ten Commandments is supposed to be engraved, and the box i which the tablet is contained. The Tsilat or the tablet by itself can also be called Tabot. The theme of the Tabot is one of the great prominent facts of the Kibre Nagast.[1] – BY Getachew Haile – A history of Tabot of Atronesa Mariam, Ethiopia – page 1.

Washington post and the Ark
Feb/10/2002

Though every one believes that the Ark of Covenant, the most precious artifact on earth, has positioned in Ethiopia for the last three thousand years, there is strange news that the Ark was stolen by the British and was taken out of Ethiopia in the last part of the nineteenth century, but now has been returned to Ethiopia. Whatever; herewith is recorded in the Washington Post on February 10/2002.

Africa

Ethiopia Reclaims Church Relic

Addis Ababa, Ethiopia

Hundreds of Ethiopians lined Addis Ababa's streets to greet the return of a replica of the Ark of the Covenant taken from Ethiopia by the British soldiers more than 130 years ago.

Government officials, diplomats, priests, and deacons from Ethiopia's Orthodox Church dressed in flowing ecclesiastical robes, collected the sacred tabot at the Bole International Airport after it has flown from London. Tabots are sacred replicas of the Ark of Covenant, which the Israelites used to carry the Ten Commandments as they traveled to the Promise land from Egypt.

Abuna Paulos, patriarch of the Ethiopian Oethodox Church, said the arrival of the six inch long carved wood tabot was the first victory in the Churches long campaign for the return of Ethiopian treasures looted by the British forces. The treasures were seized from Maqdella in 1868 after the British troops sacked the royal settlement. The loot included solid gold crowns, the tabot and manuscripts.

The Washington Post explains that this Ark was the one made by Moses, but stolen by the British from Ethiopia and finally returned to Ethiopia. So this is fresh and tangible evidence which portrays that Ethiopia possesses the Ark of Covenant, the most precious in the world.

The stone Tablet

In the Old Testament the law of God was written on stone tablet. According to the Book of Exodus Chapter 24 verse 3, in the time of Moses, people of Israel first agreed in one voice to obey God. Ever since 1350 B.C. Israelites and those people who believe in God since two thousand years ago show their agreement and obedience accordingly to the law given by God on the Book of Exodus Chapter 20 verses from 1-7.

According to Bernhard W.Anderson the law of God is divided into two. These are:1) conditional laws and 2) Absolute laws. Conditional law has characterstic feature of 'ifs and buts.' That is, it might say:" if this happens then by law this will happen to you." Absolute law is strict. You have no ifs or buts. Take for example the 1st of the Ten Commandments. It is absolute law. It just says:" I am YHWH your God you shall have no other gods before me."

Tabernacle of the Lord

In the New Testament man is the tabernacle of the Lord. This shows that a man who obeys God is a righteous man. His heart is the tablet. You can read the man who obeys God as he walks talks and lives. Therefore; man is the Ark of God. In the book of Acts 7:48 Luke writes that God does not dwell in temples made by hands.

Paul has clearly shown in 1st Corn. 3:16 that the actual dwelling place of God is in the body of the true believers, which is collectively called the Church. The Church prepares Spiritual people for Christ. The thing is when we believe in the God Al-Mighty, the Lord dwells in our physical body. Our body becomes the residence for God. This is the proper vessel of God.

Adam before he sinned was the tabernacle of God. But Adam when he went against God, he was not any more the tabernacle of God. So it is good if we do every thing according to the word of God. If we do not do according to His will we are chasing winds. If we want to live accordinhg to His will we have to read the word of God. Young children are good example. In traditional Ethiopia young children seek God Al-Mighty. So they attend Church Schools as we are going to see in detail here below.

Chapter 4
Wisdom of Traditional School students

Ethiopian Artists

There are many artists and painters in Ethiopia. Most of the indigineous paintings and art work are Church oriented. This is because through out the age's Church school students have contributed a lot in painting pictures and in drawing arts in Ethiopia. Among the Ethiopian indigineous painters, Afework Tekle is most respected for his wonderful works. Tekle's paintings are widely found in most Ethiopian and international museums.

Church School Student የቆሉ፡ተማሪ

Belief in the Lord is an unquestionable trust in God. This is why the Bible says that faith is the substance of things hoped for, the evidence of things not seen.
(Source: Hebrews 11:1)

Just trusting the Lord, the traditional Church school student goes out on foot to learn the Word of God to far off lands so many hundreds of miles away from his home He carries nothing with him. His only desire or his hunger and thirst have been always the Word of God. One cannot demonstrate such a strong and burning desire in a laboratory. This is just a willing to accept God as his creator and a willing to learn the Bible as a book of the promise of God. (See: Hebrew 4:12, Mark 13:31, Psalm 33:6 Proverbs-. 30:5-6) Hereafter, let us see how heathen Ethiopia who strongly believes in the Ark of Covenant is hungry for the Word of God.

Once a boy in Ethiopia tastes the word of God, nothing prevents him from learning more about it. The word of God is very sweet as Ezekiel explains on Chapter 3 verse 3 of his book. So this is why when a boy in traditional Ethiopia wants to know more about the Bible, first and foremost he asks information about a good Church school. After he knows something about the school, he leaves his home informing his parents. When he leaves he is a teenager, a growing boy who does not know where he goes, who does not know what he will eat, and who does not know where he will stay. In spite of all this and with no fear of wild animals, which might be waiting ahead of him, he just walks away to far off lands, leaving behind all the opportunity of living better life with his parents.

In spite of the probability that he would die, he just goes away to learn the Bible, carrying no food, clothes and with no knowledge of his future shelter. The moment he leaves, there would no be report of his success or failure to his parents. No telephone, no letter writing, no cars or any other means of communication. What his mother thinks is also positive and that she just says daily, my son has gone! "He has gone to learn: "Then a year will pass with no news. Two, three, four, five, six, seven, eight, nine and ten years will pass, with no news. And still the mother says: "My son has gone. He has gone to learn the Word of God." But her neighbors whisper, talking to each other in secret:

ተማሪው፡ በሞተ፡ በሰባት፡አመቱ

"The student died seven years ago.

ተምሮ፡ይመጣል ፡ትላለች፡ ዕናቱ፡፡

But mother says:''my son will come after graduation.''

Now let us also see the chances of such boys after post graduation. Apparently education in Tabot Christianity is restricted only to boys. Apart from the tradition, continuing education the way I mentioned above is very difficult. Continuing education is something that only strong boys could withstand. Take for example the brief demonstration the way students collect their daily bread, free of charge from the village, in the form of carry out!' It is not an easy thing. It is evidently followed by confrontation of massifs, or big dogs, which hide at the corner of each residential yard. Dogs are domestic animals intended to watch homes. They are trained for hunting. Even if they are not trained, they learn how to attack from the older dogs.

Dogs do not only learn from older dogs but they also know naturally how to attack in unity. When one barks, the other arrives from a corner. When two or three of them roam around barking in the neighborhood, they control the whole area. It is in such times that they kill lions and hyenas and tear such a student into shreds when he begs for a piece of bread.

To defend such fierce dogs, the boy has to carry a big baton or [dulla in Amharic] hiding under his clothes. If in case the dog smells or suspects of the hidden stick, he would bite the young boy. If in case the boy tries to run away, the scene of the theatre is horrible. The situation becomes worse. When the dog is aware of the fear of the student, it is bold enough to roam around the boy, to run to and fro and after checking the student's fear he tears him into shreds.

Before the introduction of modern education, unit the early part of 1920's, Church was running education. This was a transition time where by Church took the responsibility of servicing the state and the ecclesiastical matters at the same time. In that transition period the Church was also working on behalf of the Ministry of education.

Still the traditional student had a hard time. He attends classes wandering in his spare time from village to village, begging for a piece of bread for survival."

Meaning:-

የድሮ፡ተማሪ፡፡፡ትምህርት፡የሚማረው፡
ሙንደር፡ዕየዞረ፡ዕየለመነ ፡ ነው፡

When the student goes out to beg for a piece of injera/bread, he carries in one of his hands a bag for holding the food and on the other a stick to defend himself against a barking dog.

Meaning:-

ኮፋዳውን ይዞ፡
በትር፡ ተመርኩዞ፡

In Ethiopia people feed dogs giving away a portion from whatever they eat. So when the student arrives at a house in the village, the dog starts to bark assuming that the student might take away its portion. The dog has done nothing wrong. It barks to prevent the student from getting some food. This is a natural phenomenon. This is also true in human history. It is the piece of bread/ or land / business which causes warfare and enemity among man in many places of the world.

Meaning:-

ተማሪ፡ሲመጣ፡ይደነፋል ፡ውሻ
የሚወስድ፡መስሎት፡ ተሜ፡ የሱን ፡ድርሻ።
ሰውን፡ትአጣላለች፡ ይቺ፡ ትንሽ፡ ቁርሻ።

Mr. Tikuye attends traditional school

Mr. Tikuye was one of those students who passed through such experience. Trusting the Lord, Mr. Tikuye went away from his home to learn the Word of God many hundreds of miles away when he was fourteen years old. When he went out to search for the best traditional school he carries nothing with him. His only desire and hunger was just the Word of God.

When Mr. Tikuye went away leaving behind his parents he did not know about his future school or where he was heading for or what he would eat or where he would reside when he goes to school. Leaving every thing behind he went to Gojjam province where best traditional schools were located.

In Gojjam when he attended classes no one supported him because his parents who live in Wollo/ Yejju were, in a remote area. Apart from that in those days since in those days there was no any sort of transportationm one had to walk several hundred miles for months. Since he had to find his own food and residence, he was forced to wander through out the villages around his traditional school. When he wandered from one village, he had to fight against dogs. Down here is a picture that is drawn by Mr Tikuye how Church students fight against dogs when they beg for a piece of bread to continue their education.

A traditional student fighting against a dog when he begs for a piece of bread in residential areas

Wisdom

According to Proverb 1:7, ''Fear of the Lord is the beginning of wisdom.'' Or in Amharic / የጥበብ: መጀመሪያ: ዕግዚአብሄርን: መፍራት: ነው::/ This shows that a traditional student is God- fearing, wise and creative in his life. Doyou want to be god-fearing, wise and creative in your life? If you want to be god-fearing, wise and creative in your life if you read the Bible many miracles will happen in your life.

And remember!

Wisdom is from God.

God is also love.

Tikuye the Sculptor

This is a statue made by Mr. Tikuye. He is the sculptor of a statue. In the photo his family members have accompanied him. Can you identify the statue in the photo above? The 3rd person from the left is the statue whose nick name is Mr Mesele Tikuye. The 4th person from the left is Mr. Tikuye himself. The photo was taken in 1966. All the other picures are the family of Mr. Tikuye. But Mr. Mesele is a statue. The sculptor of the statue was Mr.Tikuye. He made the statue to teach students how to be a sculuptor. For himself, Mr. Tikuye did not go to school and learned how to be a sculptor. But just by creativity he made the statue, and put it in the school copmpound on "Parents' Day." On that day people were greeting the staue and saying: "Hi! Mr.Tikuye! " They greeted the statue, because the statue looked like him.

Underneath the statue, Tikuye wrote the following in Amharic.

Let the statue speak:

Meaning:

ሐውልቱ፡ ይናገር፡፡
ከውሃ፡ ከጭቃ፡ ትኩዬ፡ ሠራኝ፡
ስሜንም፡ መሰለ፡ ብሎ፡ ሰየመኝ፡፡
ዕኔን፡ የሠራብት፡ ዋና፡ ዓላማው፡
የሐውልትን፡ሥራ፡ለማስተማር፡ነው፡፡

Meaning:-

I am Tikuye made

Out of water and mud

Mesele is my name.

Because I look like him

When he made me he had a cause

To teach statue work was the purpose.

Mr. Tikuye had never been in art school. He knew how to be a sculuptor. He made a statue that resembled him. He did not go to learn about art and painting. But he was teaching about art and painting. Just by observation he was teaching students how to draw or how to paint. When he was teaching, he starts from simple and then goes on to the complex.

Introduction of Christianity into Ethiopia

Through Queen Sheba Ethiopia has known God Al-Mighty since 950 B.C. That was in the Old Testament. And about thirteen hundred years later after the death of Queen Sheba Christianity was officially introduced into Ethiopia by the 4th century A.D.

So as of the 4th century A.D., Ethiopia has been known as a Christian nation. So since that time people of Ethiopia believe in God the Father, the Son of God Jesus, and in Holy Spirit. Since the 4th century A.D. Ethiopia has been known as a Christian island.

Picture of Mr. Tikuye

So far we were talking about the drawings of Mr.Tikuye. Now herewith you can see the picture of Mr. Tikuye. He believes in in God Al-Mighty He knows that God is Spirit and since his heart is at the Cross he sings and praises in Geez language for glory of the the Lord. God has also given him wisdom to be interested in artistic work and creativity and this is why he draws Cross scrolls. Mr. Tikuye has a beautiful picture of the Cross on his hand. He tries to do every thing to the glory of God

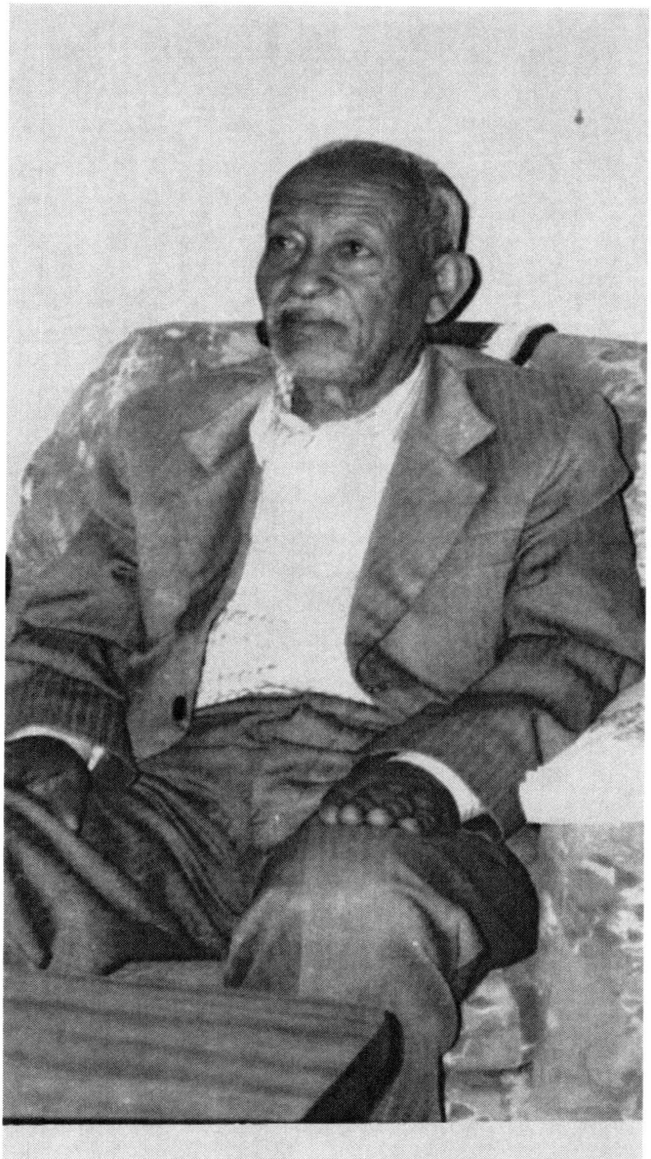

Scrolls of Tikuye

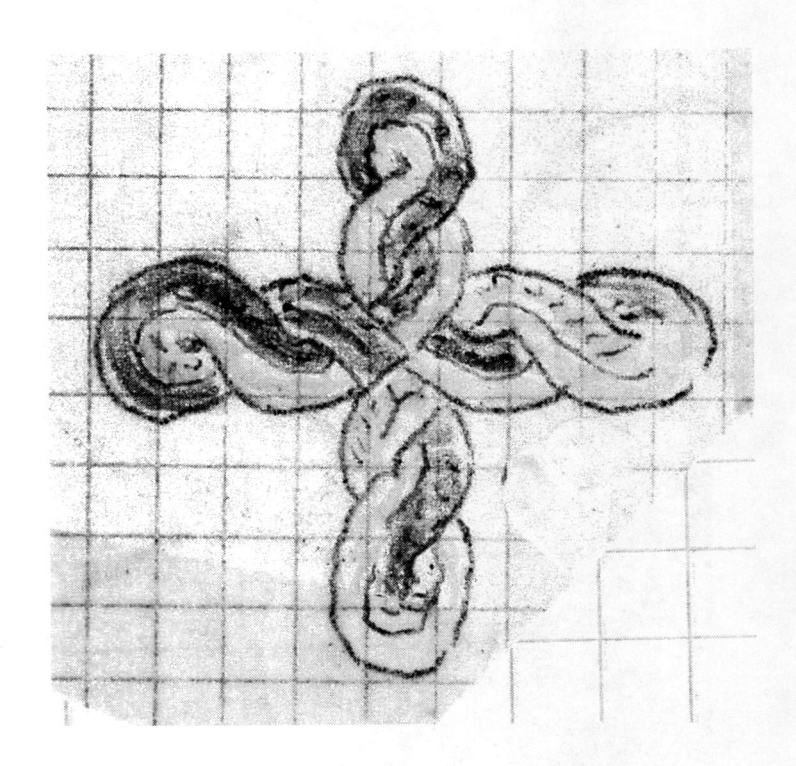

85

86

87

88

89

ሰዓሉሁ፡ ትኩዩ፡ ገብረ፡ ኢያሱ፡ ሸ
ዘብሔረ፡ ኢትዮጵያ

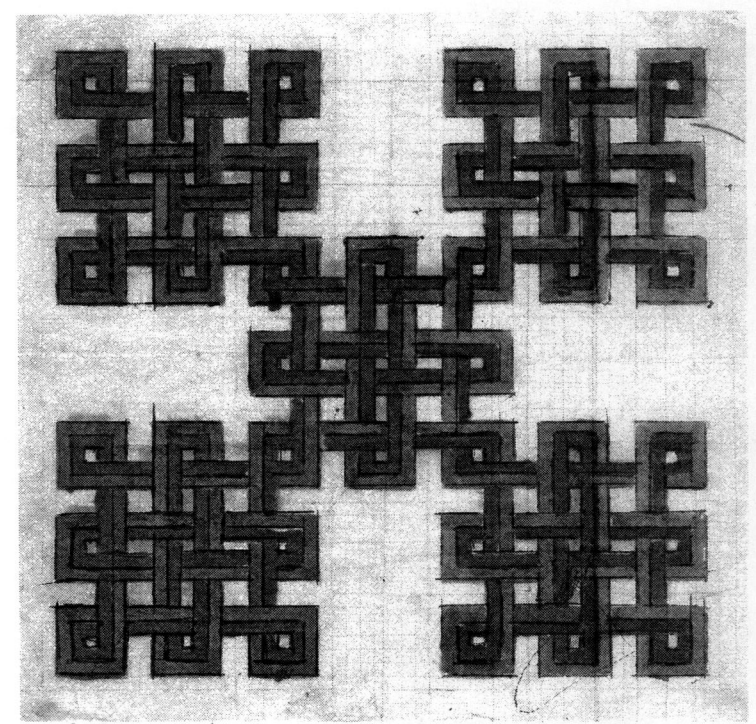

91

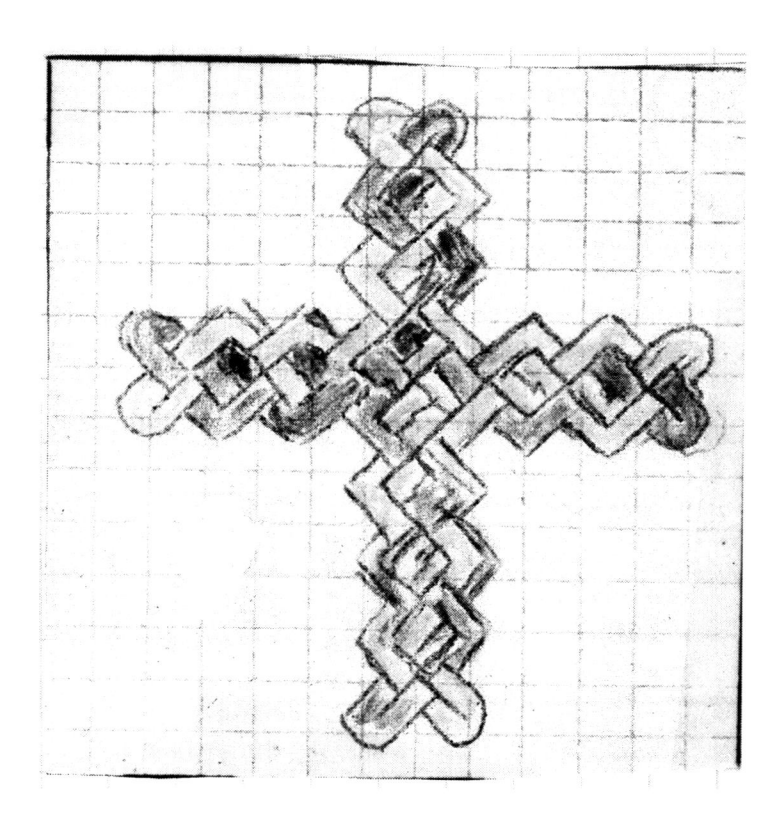

ሠዓሊው ፡ ተክሎ ገብሪ ኢየሱስ
ዘክሎሪ ኢትዮጵያ

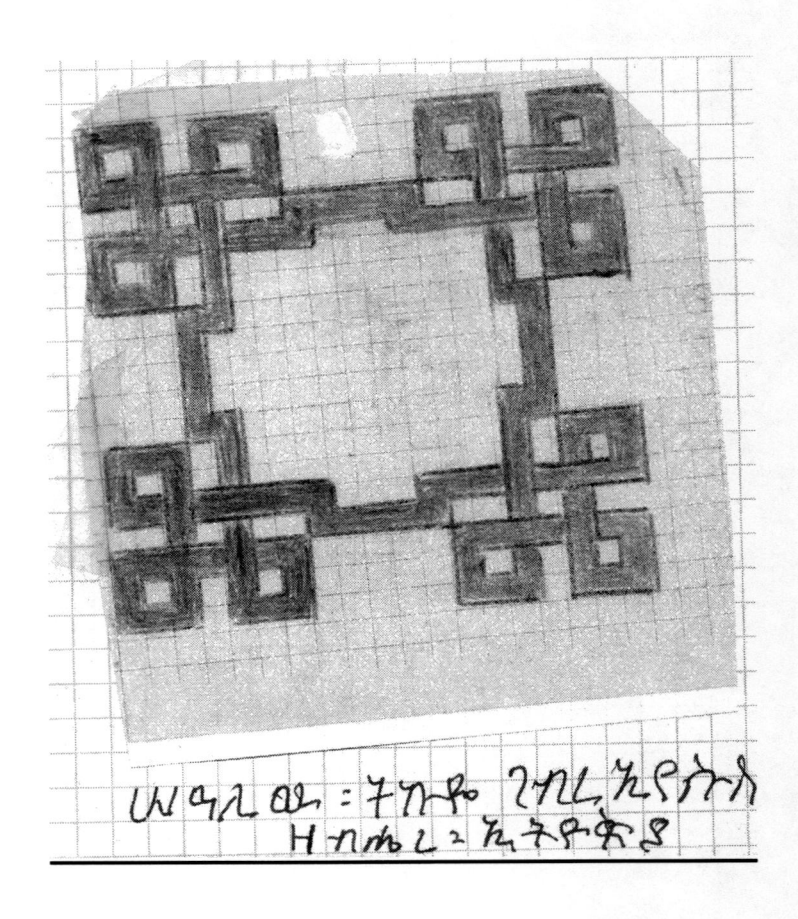

93

94

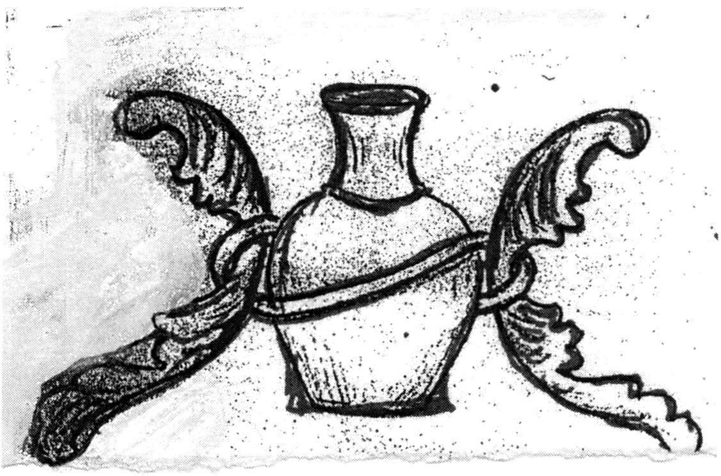

Drawn by Mr Tikuye

Writing in Ethiopia

Writing in Ethiopia has a long history. The ancient Ethiopian language was Geez. The Ethiopic language of Geez originated from an ancient language which had well developed script. This language from which Geez originated and had well developed script was the Sabean language.

The Semetic Sabean people of South Arabia were using the Sabean script about 2500 years ago. The Semetic Sabean people had a fidel sort of script called the Sabean script. Geez, the ancient Ethiopian language got the idea of fidel script from the Sabean language. So this is why Geez became the written language for Ethiopia for thousands of years and when Geez dies Amharic, Tigrigna and Oromigna became written languages taking the Geez script.

Source- – Baye Yimam- Ph. D
(Associate Professor and Head of Department of Linguistics, 1992 Addis Ababa, Ethiopia)

Geez	Sabian	Geez	Sabian	Geez	Sabian
ሀ	⊓	መ	⊙	ፀ	○
ለ	⊓	ሐ	✕	ኀ	⊓
ገ	⊐	ኅ	⊥⊥	ለ	⊐
ደ	▷	ነ	▢	ᎠᎠ	◇
ሀ	⊔	ሃ	⊥⊥	ነ	⊔
ዐ	○	ፀ	▭	ኅ	⊓
ፈ	◇	ቀ	⏊	ሠ	⋟
ጸ	⚲	ፈ	⎓	ተ	✕

Source- Kessis Kefyalew Merahi – The Contribution of Orthodox Tewahedo Church Addis Ababa, Ethiopia 1999, page 127)

A man writing on a Parchment

ሥዕሉ፡ ትንቢ፡ ገብረ፡ እየሱስ
ሀገሩ፡ ኢትዮጵያ —
— Meaning- Picture drawn by Mr Tikuye Gebre-Eyesus who is Ethiopian in nationality

    Printing press was invented by Johan Gutenberg who was a German by nationality. He first invented prnting press in 1439 A.D. Before that time Church people wrote books by hand. Now realize how people like King David, King Solomon, Apostle Paul and others wrote all these books by hand making their own parchment, ink, pen and pecils and also taking care of their administrative duties. In Ethiopia there were many books written on parchments by priests of Traditional Church schools who were called wise men or liq/ in Amharic until early 1950. Very, Very few Bible books as compared to the population of Ethiopia however, were published by the help of modern printing press in 1947 according to Ethiopian calander. So shortage of books has always been a problem to spread the Gospel in Ethiopia. This is an important thing to know if there is any one who wants to give away some of his books to Ethiopia.

    Here where ever you go in America you hold in your hand and read special books. You don't even mind how these books were written or where you get them because books are published daily and are available every where.

Long time ago in every part of the world books was very few. This was because the books were written by hand. To finish writing a book it took several years. This was because pen and pencils were made by hand.

The black ink was made by mixing different types of leaves of plants like kitikita, kerete, bamboo, horn of a sheep, the shekona of an ox. The red ink was also made by mixing red soil with the fruit of berry, the flower of feheso, mencherero enchet, red flowers and much more. One cannot just mix all these. Ink making has its own process according to Kessis Merahi. (Source Kessis Kefya according to Kessis Kefyalew Merahi, page 147)

The paper used for writing was also called parchment. It was made by hand from goat skin. In Amharic it is called Birana/ ብራና፡፡/ After it was written it goes to the book binder. It was done with dry tendon of oxen. In Amharic it means: መጽሃፉ፡ከተጻፈ፡በሁዋላ፡ደግሞ፡መጠረዝ፡አለበት፡፡የሚጠረዘውም፡በበሬ፡ጅማት፡ነበር፡፡

Ancient People

Ancient prophets of Israel seemed to have written books of the Old Testament on parchments by hand. There was no printing press at that time. More than half, to be specific /fourteen of the 27 of of the New Testament books were also written by Apostle Paul. It seemed that he might have written all these books on parchments. He wrote all these books according to Church history probably from 50 B.C. until he dies as a martyr of Christ in 67 B.C. Knowledge of date helps to make approximate time. So it seems that he wrote all these books by hand making his own ink, and pen, preaching the Gospel at the same time to the Gentiles, planting Churches everywhere he goes, settling down disputes among Church members, working for his food, bitten by his foes, who were ambushing in thick forests of those days, writting letters to his brothers in Christ, teaching the gospels in Churches and Bible studies, being arrested and put into jails several times.

We have got many things from Israel. There is nothing that we did not get from Israel. We have learned how to write on parchment making ink and pen out of wild plants. The Bible itself is from Israel. Jesus Himself was revealed to the people of Israel. All this is to show that Ethiopia making close relationship with Israel had known God Himself. Learning from the people of Israel Ethiopia through out the ages has preserved the Bible writing on parchments.

Chapter 5

Church and State
Ethiopian Capitals

According to multiple evidences the 1st capital city of Ethiopia was Axum. From Axum the capital moved to Lasta-Lalibela. From Lalibela the capital moved to Gondar. From Gondar it moved to Dabra Tabor. From Dabra Tabor it moved to Entoto. From Entoto, it moved to Finifine. It is now called Addis Ababa which means "*NewFlower.*"

The new city, Addis Ababa was established after the Ethiopian Empire state was consolidated. In all these cities when people of Ethiopia eat or drink or do anything else they did it to honor God AlMighty according to first Corinthians Chapter 10:31. That is, in every city God was glorified. In all of these cities nobles had built many Churches. In all of these cities there were many priests. Explorers and travellers of 1500, 1600, 1700, 1800, 1900 and 2000 A.D. have written that Ethiopia was/ is a country of priests and Churches. Take for example when the capital of Ethiopia was in the city of Lalibela, one of the 8th wonders, the rock-hewn Church of Lalibela was built. Take Gonder another example, which was/is city of priests and Churches.

As mentioned above at 1st Addis Ababa was called New Flower. The founder of New Flower in 1880's was Empress Taitu. Addis Ababa has been the capital city of Ethiopia for over a century. Through out the ages the unity of Ethiopia has been strong. This was true even in the Era of Princes. Ethiopia was under the era of diiferent rival regional leaders for one hundred thirty years. The Era of Princes / Zemene Mesafint began in the last quarter of the 18th century. In the Era of Princes, nobles of the provinces were divided and were fighting against each other. This portrays that there was political inadequacy. Because of that there was fighting against each other frequently. While they were fighting against each other Kassa of Quarra emerged suddenly and destroyed this political anarchy. So the Era of Princes ended in the last quarter of the 19th century with the rise of Kassa of Quarra and became Emperor Theodore II.

After the end of the Zemene Mesafint reunification of Ethiopia started by Emperor Theodore II. His capital was at Maqdella in Wollo. After the Napir expedition and death of Emperor Theodore/ Atse Tewodros, unification of Ethiopia continued pretty well under Emperor Yohannes IV. When Empeor Yohannes IV was assassinated at the battle of Metema, fighting against the Sudanese Emperor Menilik II came to power. After the death of Minilik II, Lij Iyassu IV came to power. After Queen Zawditou, Emperor Haile Selassie I came to power. Emperor Haile Selassie I strongly united and modernized Ethiopia making his capital city at Addis Ababa. When Emperor Haile Selassie I was assassinated by members of the derg military junta backed by the Russians, political crisis, civil war and elements to weaken Ethiopia came one after the other. This happened because the power of this big powerful country became under the control selfish leaders.

The military supported by Russia, started to propagate that it will liberate people from harsh rule. They blew their false wind of proclamation of equality, fraternity and liberty. False propagation takes nowhere. Giving their deaf ears to the population, puppets of Russia built for themselves 'the tower of Babel' according to Genesis 11:1-9. In those few and miserable years supporters of the regime became rich and powerful at the expense of the innocent people. Every thing one does badly kills him finally. Nobody in the world prevents that from happening. So when the the regime lost popular support false propagation did not work and its downfall became imminent. This is an all time lesson for whosoever takes power and abuse people. Whatever goes up comes down. It is a matter of time. This is the situation and the consequence. But still no body seems ready to learn from previous stories of mankind.

With in the seventeen years of the Derg's rule intellectuals of Ethiopia were wiped out totally. History records that these patriots died burned with fire of nationalism. In the mean time the new regime came to power supported mainly by peasants, red terror run away youth, and military captives and other section of the population.

Seek God's leadership

Leaders who listen to the guidance and instruction of the Lord are smart leaders. People who elect leaders praying in the name of Jesus are wise. What ever the condition might be it is good to follow what the Lord says.

So let us see things in this way. Seeking the leadership of the Lord is the 4th element of leadership according to my assumption. The rest of the three are mentioned herewith and you know them. Going out from our box let us see how Lord's leadership is superior of all. This is because His leadership gives guidance and instruction to each of the three types of leadership. In fact leaders in each of the three styles of leadership become leaders with the will of God. If this is true these leaders when they come to power they are supposed to glorify God. Why? Because they get the power with His will and they would loose their power with His will.

The three types of leadership that we talk about are democracy, authoritative and laissez-faire.

1) Democracy

People enjoy freedom of speech, religion and political opinion in this type of government. Source- dictionary * People say:"It is a good one." Americans enjoy democracy. This is because they respect the law of their country and work hard for the development of their economy and for the survival of their democracy. Leaders are just in power to serve the people and when their term is over they leave their power with joy with out making any mess.

As we saw above America is a good example of a country which enjoys democracy. When Senator McCain for example lost the vote for presidency on November 4/ 2008 he made a good speech that touches the heart of all Americans because his heart was on the future of America and not on himself. He was happy when Senator Obama won and became elect president. He expressed his good wishes for Obama and his leadership. This is a good lesson for leaders who believe in democracy and who wish to apply it for the benefit of the whole population under their domain.

1) የዲሞክራሲ:አመራር::

የንግግር:የመብት:የሃይማኖትና:ህሳብን:የመግለጽ:ነጻነት:ያለበት: ጥሩ:አመራር: ነው::

2) *An authoritarian type of government*

Under authoritarian type of government the leader requires obedience from the people:- Source- dictionary. People say:"This leadership is ruthless and poisonous like snake."- He considers his subjects as slaves.

2 የአምባገነን:አመራር:-

ሥልጣን:ማሳያ:

አመራር::ዕምብዛም:ክፉ:ሲሆን:ሰወች:ዕባብ:ነው:

ይናደፋል:ይሉና:ይጠሉትአል::

አምባገነንነቱ:ሲበዛ:ክፉ:ስትሆን:ህይሉን:ያሳይ:ጀመር:

ይሉን:ቅራኔ:ያሳዩሃል::

3) Laissez - faire

Laissez – faire allows business. Under this type of government business runs with little or no government interfirance. (Source –dictionary)

Under the leadership of laissez – faire type of government, because the leader is very nice people want to lick it like honey, says Dr. Yalew Engedayehu, Professor of Addis Abeba University

3   የሌዜዝፌር፡ አመራር

ሥራን

ሰዎች፡ዕንደልባቸው፡መሪ፡ላይቆጣጠራቸው፡በጸነት፡ ሚያከህዱበት፡አመራር፡ነው፡፡ነገር፡ግን፡ዕምብዛም፡ ደግ፡ሲሆን፡ ሰዎች፡ ማር፡ ነው፡ ብለው፡ ይልሱትአል፡፡

According to Psalm 20:7-9, leaders who rely on chariots and horses with out trusting God crumble easily and quickly while those who trust the Lord become strong and popular. Take for example Israel. Israel believed in Al- Mighty God since ancient times. God was their leader. In those days Israel was peaceful and strong.

Nonetheless since Israel is the Promise land of God it is strong and victorious through out the Aages. Take another example Ethiopia. The Solomonic line was also ruling in Ethiopia giving glory to Al-Mighty God for thousands of years until the monarchy was overthrown in early 1970's.

Since the overthrow of the monarchy Ethiopia tried different types of leaderships. But Ethiopia seems to be disasatisfied with any of them. Hence now Ethiopia seeks God's mercy, guidance and protection. The people turn their face to Emanuel believing that He is the right Master that can guide in the right way. People in general believe that He is Lord of lords and King of kings that can give power and strength to the weak.

God keeps the border

Rich people depend on their money. Powerful people depend on their soldiers. It is natural for people to depend by what they have. That happens. We see it. It is a way of life. Believers also depend on the Lord because He is the source of their joy according to John 7:38. Powerful people have weapons to depend on. Believers empty handed but full of faith in their heart depend on the Lord. Here comes the difference. In times of war however; when believers just stay with Jesus with out fear as the enemy comes forward to attack them, see what happens.

When the enemy sees believers standing with Jesus with out fear, the enemy itself backs away and falls to the ground instantly. See John 18:6. Why? This is because the Lord Al-Mighty is on their side. Take another example David the Shepherd and Goliath. David killed Goliath with out a weapon and it was at that time according Psalm 91:8. It was at this time that David saw with his own eyes the punishment of the wicked and proved that the life of a believer is a life of victory. Because the life of Christians is a life of victory they sing a song of victory saying:

"When the Ocean rises
And the thunder roars
I will soar over the the storm
Jesus is the King over the flood."

Source:-Choir Song of Immanuel Church, 16819 New Hampshire Ave. Silver Spring Md. 20905.

Like Goliath non-believers always plan to attack. A non-believer intends to attack his enemy with a weapon. According to Matthew 26: 52, Christians like King David believe that any one who lives by fighting will die by fighting. So Christians stay away from physical fighting. They just stay with Jesus and fight spiritually. When they fight spiritually God is in control of the situation. Take also the main land of Israel. Ethiopia too depending on the Lord has been preserved by the power of God Al-Mighty enjoying glorious eras of peace with out well trained national army boasting about her three thousands of years of independence. For example with out a national army in 1896 at the battle of Adwa got victory over Italy, one of the powerful countries of Europe. Here I don't mean there should not be an army. A country must have a strong army together with most recent weapons. But the army should not be used for aggression and invasion. For example Ethiopia lost victory when she organized one million strong in 1970's and 80's, built up modern sophisticated weapons and bombarded with jets her own civilians with out wisdom. The rest is written in Ethiopian history. የቀረውስ፡ በኢትዮጵያ፡ ትአሪክ፡ ተጽፎ፡የለምን፡፡?

As recorded in Amos 9:9 when people turn their back from the Lord, they are sifted or shaked by God as corn is sifted in a sieve. God is good. He sifts His people to make them good. ''Sifting method of God'' separates sin from good work. When sin is gone they start to praise. Satan does not sift. He is powerless. He can only deceive if he finds a person who does not call the name of Jesus or a person who does not praise. Especially those people who claim themselves as people of God and who are not ready to call the name of Jesus are losers in the war-field that is waged by Satan. They lose the war because the devil knows how to deceive them. Decieving is a trick that the devil uses according to the Book of Ephesians Chapter 6:10-11. Nonetheless; if any one wants to fight against the evil effectively like that of a mighty Roman soldier he should put on all the armor that God gives him because it is when one wears the armor of God that he can defend himself against the Devil's tricks according to the Book of Ephesians Chapter 6.

God sifts His people. He sifts them for their own good. Sifting method is a means to separate the good from the bad. Sifting method is also used mostly by farmers who want to separate the wheat/ the good /from the chaff/ the bad. Take also another example and that is taking out butter from cow milk. In Ethiopia a lady in the farm shakes the milk in a container. After that she gets butter. The Ethiopian butter is wonderful. People who grow in the farm know how sweet it is to eat fresh bread after separating the wheat from the chaff. Also how wonderful it is to live as a borne again Christian. Those who leave the Adam nature behind know many things. They have passed through many things that tried to shake their lives.

Actually when one passes through a storm he should not complain. To pass through a storm and to be shaked in his time of trouble is good for life. So when God shakes you in the march of life down the road don't shake, fear or complain. It is always for good to pass through a storm, because when you pass through the strorm Immanuel is with you and if Immanuel is with you, who is against you?

Life is extremely hard for the majority of Ethiopians today. This might be God's season of sifting His people and His will to turn to them and bless them. It is true that when the Lord gets angry He sifts. He does not like disobedience. If the people of God disobey the Lord it is curse. God sifts them with the plan to turn them back and not punish according to Deuteronomy Chapter 28. It is also true that when the Lord gets angry and sifts His people Satan holds in his hand the fan thinking that this will increase the suffering and shaking of God's people. At this time however; God's people should never get angry about the works of Satan. The devil has no power. Besides he does not at all understand the plan God has for His people. God is good all the time. He sifts His people to bring back their old good days and their old good ways.

When the Lord sifts His people, believers should never feel desperate or show impatient or any sort of murmer. In hard times believers should always stay praying and sanctifying themselves so that God would bring back the old good days and the old good ways. It is when believers are clean from sin that it is possible to get victory over Satan. It is when believers come closer to God that they can rebuke Satan in the name of Jesus according to John 16:23. It is when believers sanctify themselves that they can live peacefully. For those who sanctify themselves Jesus gives authority to set themselves free from the threat of Satan. Congrdulation! Lord our God is faithful. He never changes or changes His mind. By the Blood of the Lamb and by the word of their testimony Satan is already defeated. The war is over. See - Revelation 12:11.

For those who are not clean the promise of God does not work. Satan does not understand the secret why God sifts

His people. The Lord sifts His people because He wants to purify and preserve them and not to destroy them. Food is preserved from being spoiled by bacteria in a frigid for a short time. Man is preserved from being spoiled by reading the Word of God and by worshipping and praising the Lord Himself.

Jesus preserves believers from being spoiled from the virus of Satan forever – To understand this in detail; you can see the book of Jude especially verse 24:25. You can also have a glance at the story of the Israelites when they had close intimacy with the Lord in the time of Exodus. Though God is a consuming fire, He is also compassionate. After the Israelites broke their Covenant with the Lord and made the 'Golden Calf,' through the prayer and mediation of Moses God was merciful to them according to Exodus 33:19. This teaches us individually and as a nation to turn to Al- Mighty Lord all the time.

National Movement Of Fasting and Praying

In the world we live in everybody has an origin or an ancestry. So it is human nature to think of his origin. Even if one does not care to know where he is from, people will ask him where he is from. If there is a person who does not care to know where he is from, this is an isolated and a strange thing.

For many people the question of their origin is a sensitive issue. For those who know their origin pretty well national self conciousness/ national feeling/ is a key factor that leads them to think deeply in remembrance of their past. Take Moses for example. God has a plan for every one. He also knows knows where everyone is from. When God wants to do something for some one or for a given country no one will stop him. For example; God used Moses because He knows where Moses is from. So saving Moses from death in his childhood He raised him and prepared him for the future struggle against the Pharoah. So after making Moses the commander in chief for the war front God started the national movement to liberate the people of Israel. That movement or liberation front in the Bible is called Exodus. According to Promise Bible the word 'Exodus'- comes from the Greek word meaning – 'Going out.' In the modern time one must also 'go out' in order to liberate oppressed people. It was through the principle of 'Exodus' or ''Going out'' that God sets free the people of Israel from slavery.

Consequently; by the help of God; therefore, people of Israel dreamt to do good and to fight and to liberate themselves. So to fight for your people is a good. God Himself used it for the people of Israel. So there is nothing wrong to support your people when your people are really oppressed. It is always good to stand at the side of the hopeless. Hopeless is homeless. Many people in history had done it for their original homeland. People might die by by typhoid suddenly. But to die for the good of mankind is worthy. It is also worthy if one has the money with out hidden motive to build industries; schools, hospitals, roads and the like for his country. In the history of mankind national movement usually refers to wars waged against enemies that attack a given geographical territory. What has been discussed so far is all done out of a national feeling.

If a nation does not defend its boundary enemies will colonize it. If it is colonized it will lose its freedom. Losing its freedom it will fall into slavery of the invading power. The devil comes to us to throw us in different ways. We do not have enemies in the world we live in. Our enemy is Satan himself and according to the Book of Ephesians, Chapter 6, we are fighting against the rulers of darkness.

Fasting and praying are the best weapons that pierce and break into pieces any enemy force. So if we fast and ask God to do good things for your country, He will do it. For example Elijah prayed after a long drought in Israel for rainfall. So the Lord blessed Elijah sending rain toover Israel. If you fast and pray and ask God, He will also do it for your nation if you sincerely fast.

If you want to save your humble country people from suppression or oppression just ask the Lord praying and crying. What you do is a simple thing. What you have to do is to kneel down, in your home at a certain corner and to send the bullets of prayer into the open air. In the name of God what ever you do is secret. So just do it secretly and he Lord will do the rest. If you send prayer with tears, the bad things in your body system will be cleansed and it is when the bad things in your body system will be washed away pretty well and your prayer will work effectively. It is also when your prayer is effective that your prayer crosses rivers, mountains, valleys and plains, and penetrates through the walls of the enemy house and bomard him where he is. We learn that these weapons are strong because we always read in history books that fasting and praying have been used through out the ages. Since fasting and praying is from God and the architect is God Himself people who pray can dismiss any powerful fortress at any time. To confirm that your prayer is answered ask the Lord for confirmation. That confirmation will help you to grow in the Spirit of the Lord. It ends there. And one should also know that the Spirit of the Lord is not given for power mongers.

If people in a given country turn to the Lord it is a spiritual and wonderful national movement. But Satan does not like such a thing. When one turns to God he opens his door of prayer. This is because when one opens his door of prayer blessing will come into his house. But Satan does not like to see anyone's door of prayer open. Whether the devil likes it or not Christians must open their door of prayer. Also they should repent, confess their sins, fast and pray frequently and should wait to see what the Lord would do opening their doors of prayer.

Ethiopia is one of the Christian nations in which the devil roams around her to devour her. Since it is a Christian nation, evil spirit initiates non-believers to hinder her progress through closing their doors of prayer. The same is true for other Christian nations too. The devil is against the people of God in general. He is also everywhere. The devil is in Ethiopia. It is in Israel watching to attack. Israel is passing through difficulties, because it is a Promise Land. But God has designed these countries to pass through the storm that the devil arranges. Whenever; therefore when the devil wants to throw believers into storm Jesus stops that terrible storm according to the Book of Mark 4:35-41. Besides that the Lord has given the power of allowing and not allowing doing the same for man himself as mentioned herewith saying:

"I promise you that God in heaven will allow whatever you allow on earth, but He will not allow anything, you don't allow." See Matthew 18:18. Besides whenever two or three of you come together in my name, I am there with you," the Lord says on Matthew 18:20. Therefore this shows that coming closer to God is a movement to fight Satan. Since God does not neglect even a single man, He answers prayers to dismiss the plan of the evil spirit. This portrays that this evidence is supported by the word of God. According to the Bible if two or three agree about some thing on earth for what they pray, God in heaven will do it for them. This is why we need to pray for Israel, for the nations, for Ethiopia and for America. The greater the storm upon these nations, the more they will be successful if believers pray according to Matthew 18:19. This shows that when believers pray for the nations they will bring solution.

Many nations have had many national movements. That is great. National fronts fight against enemies that come to mess up national integrity. In times like this national fasting, praying and worshipping the Lord helps to establish strong relationship with God and to maintain national consolidation. This movement is spiritual. It is strong because it has Al-Mighty power, on the side of the movement. So coming close to Al-Mighty power all believers have to pray and earnestly ask God to work together with them. So people have to pray. Praying is a cause to win 100% in legislative elections, to develop and raise National Gross Product, health, and education to the maximum.

To give some thing to others in the name of Jesus with smiling face and with legacy is one of the master keys to go to heaven. To give tithes and offerings to the Church and obedience to the Lord and devoted worship are means and ways to collect a large harvest and a means to go out of poverty. Church teaches that to give is an easy way to become rich. Church also teaches that praying and giving is the way to go to heaven. So if people give poverty has no chance of survival. A person who gives can be successful. The more, one gives the richer he will be. So if people of poor nations become loyal to the Lord and give their tithes to spread the gospel they will become rich from time to time. There is no other way for people than becoming Christian and serving the Lord-God, because this is the only way to become healthy and wealthy and a means to live peacefully.

Even in the natural world when you give, many friends will escort you. If you do not give people will think that there is glue in your hand and will run away from you. This is a natural phenomenon. So you have to give. In the Spiritual world also if you do not give you are running away from shower of blessings of the Lord. Whenever; you are not willing to give, do not think that you are smart. It is not scriptural. Besides that you know that you are not happy internally. But the moment you give you know that your body relaxes and is ready to worhip. There is no good confirmation than this. According to the Bible it is true that when people pay their thithes to their local Church, God will open the windows of heaven to pour prosperity for His people according to the Book of Malachi Chapter 3.

For a carnal minded person to give some money to spread the gospel is a foolish thing. For a spiritual person giving is a source of blessing because he/ she believes in the theory of sow and reap. Take for example Matthew 6:14-15. According to Matthew 6:14-15:''If you forgive others for the wrongs they do to you, Your Father in heaven will forgive you. But if you do not forgive others, your Father will not forgive your sins. '' This is great because just for forgiving others your Father in heaven forgives your sins. To know what the Lord expects from us is wonderful. It helps us to sow the best seed and to collect the best harvest. This theory is time tested and biblically proved. On the other hand if you doubt this theory of sow and reap your life will be jeopardized and once it is jeopardized it is hard to fix it. If people understand the theory of sow and reap they will be $100^0/^0$ successful in life. This needs a great national movement so that every one will be successful in life. Herewith, there are more examples and you can have a glance at them.

* If you are open for others wisely, you will have many intimate friends.
* If you are honest for others, many will trust you and respect

you.
* If you committe sin, the price of sin is death.
* If you are greedy you will gain nothing.
* If you are bitter every body will hate you and run away.
* If you work hard you will earn more.
* If you have faith in the Lord you will see miracles.

Pending the above as is, let us talk about tourists when they visit Ethiopia. Tourists like to travel to Ethiopia. This is because they know that Ethiopia is a tourist paradise. Missionaries like to trave to Ethiopia because they know that the Lord who gives them authority to make disciples goes with them according to Matthew 28:19-20, and when the Lord goes with missionaries according to the Book of Matthew He reveals Himself to tourists for it is His will to save every one who opens his heart to Him.

Furthermore; both tourists and missionaries when they come to Ethiopia they are eager to know about the history, geography, the people, the culture and tradition of this ancient country. Knowing their desire the government of Ethiopia allows tourists and missionaries to visit the beautiful historical sites of the country and on the other hand allow them to preach the Word of God with freedom. In this case unlike the preceeding Communist government credit goes to the present government of Ethiopia for allowing missionaries and Ethiopian believers to preach in liberty.

Ethiopian believers work together in cooperation with missionaries to spread the Word. When also they pray according to the Lord's will, they receive authority from Him. When believers pray for their leaders according to 1st Timothy 2: 2, the Lord accepts their prayer for His name sake. Believers on the other hand pray for the people by and large as well. When they intercede for both the leaders and for the toiling mass they are blessed.

He who stays with the Lord feels the presence of Holy Spirit and that is a great thing. There is nothing on the universe than this. Take for example Moses. He stays with the Lord in the wilderness and as a result he came close to God. He was feeling the presence of the Holy Spirit than any other person in the world in his generation and the generations after him.

Because Holy Spirit was with Moses the people of Israel set free from Egyptian yoke. So the tactic to set free a nation is to make close relationship with God. This is a lesson which teaches how to create a nation under God. The prominent example of this promise is Israel.

When people of Israel were on wilderness, Moses stayed with the Lord on Sinai Mountain for forty days and forty nights. Finally when he comes down the mountain his face was shinning according to Exodus 34:29-30. His face was shinning because he was with God. Your face also will shine too if you stay close to God. But if you stay away from the Lord there would be a possibility that you might committe sin. When a person does not stay with the Lord, his face does not shine because sin drains away his grace.

A person who committes sin falls short of the glory of God according to Romans 3:23. But a person who has authority from God is found in the Church serving the Lord because Church represents the authority of God. So if people from the Church take their position and stay with the Lord they can drive the devil away. They drive the devil away because they have authority from God Al- Mighty. Mahesh Chanda preached in the Calvary Campground of Ashland, Virginia from June 27 – 29/ 2008, how the devil attacks nations of the world and how to drive away the devil.

Church's authority over the devil

When Church says according to James 4:7: " Submit yourselves, therefore unto God and resist the devil, he will flee from you. So when you say:" Devil! In the name of Jesus go away from the family of believers, Satan will go away!" As a result many broken families would heal. After being healed these families go in the right direction and in the will of the Lord. As a result children will be free from abortion.

Now you see how to drive away the Devil. You also on your behalf can practice how to drive the Devil away. If you have faith in God and put your faith in Jesus you can drive away the devil. As long as you stay with the Lord, Holy Spirit is with you. If Holy Spirit is with you the Devil runs away from you according to Acts 19:2. So have faith in Jesus and drive away the devil from your every thing. That is from your:

        1) Business
        2) Family
        3) Government
        4) Religeon
        5) Culture
        6) Education
        7) Finance

So drive the devil from your business saying:
* "Devil! Go away from my business!"
* "Devil! Go away from my School!"
* "Devil! Go away from my government!"
* "Devil! Go away from my belief!"
* "Devil! Go away from my finance!"
* "Devil! Go away from my family! "

People who pray for their nation are salt of their land. They drive away the devil. Take for example Moses, Joshua, King David, Elijah, King Solomon, Ezra, Nehemiah and others were the salt and light for Israel. You too, if you pray for Ethiopia you are the salt and light for this lovely land. Because you are salt of the land, when you pray God hears you. (See 1st Samuel 1:1-20.). So according to Matthew 5:16 if you are ready to make your light shine, everyone will get light. Elijah was a person like you. Samuel was a person like you. They were rich in the spirit of the Lord.

As discussed above you too have attended so many conferences and Bible studies. You have read the Bible so many times. You have attended so many conferences to be rich in the Spirit and it is certain that you are already rich in Spirit. You love the people of Ethiopia. You are the light of Ethiopia. Come on! Stand up! Ttrust the Lord and work with Him.

In any generation, in a given country God has some holy people. Ethiopia has many holy people in this generation. But the sign of holiness is when one receives message from God. Now Ethiopia wants her holy people to pray until they touch heaven and bring her a message from God. Ethiopia wants these holy people because this Christian nation believes that when holy people pray for her in the name of the Lord with their contrite heart, they will receive a message from Al-Mighty God.

First thing must come first. Whenever we need change we pray first to get message from God. With out having a message from the Lord just to brag for change, no economic, political or social development comes. Take for example the history of Ethiopia. Towards the end of 1960's and early 1970's people of Ethiopia wanted change with out having a Word from God. Simply by emotion the mob of those days wanted democracy like the rest of the world. In ancient Israel too there was the same history. Israel was ruled by prophets. The prophets were representatives of God. Samuel was the last prophet to rule Israel. When Prophet Samuel gets old the mob needed change. They wanted to be ruled by a king like the neighbouring lands. Samuel was upset and prayed. God told Samuel to do whatever they wanted to do. I am really the one whom they have rejected as their king.
(See 1ST Samuel 8:6-8.)

As mentioned above God warned Israelites through Samuel telling them the king would maltreat them and after that they would suffer the consequence. As God said after Israelites chose their leader they went from one problem to the other. This is the result of seeking change and rejection of the Lord.

Change seems good. Nonetheless; change has bad consequences as well unless handled well and is in line with the will of God. Especially when people of God want change they have to ask the Lord 1st what to do. Ethiopian history teaches us that the life of the people has always been connected with Christianity. In those years when there was strong unity between the Church and state, Ethiopia was known as a magnanimous country in Africa. But when Ethiopia gave her back to God Al-Mighty it started to decline and its Grand Era to wither away.

In early 1970's when the derg wanted change they

had a plan to establish an aetheist form of government. They had a plan to reject God. When Communism was established according to their wishes, the state officials and their followers rejected God. Rejecting God they persecuted Christians. From school curriculum they took out the name of God. After that they began to magnify the name of Communist and military leaders. Instead of glorifying God Al-Mighty, they glorified the Russian leaders and the derg officials. So death was at the door, because God was not glorified.

In ancient Israel when people wanted change, God warned them that their sons would join the army and the cavalry if they go ahead with the change they wished. He also warned them that some would be officers in charge of thousand soldiers. Others would be in charge of fifty. Still others will have to farm and harvest for the war purpose. Others wuld make weapons and parts of weapons for the war. Their daughters would do the cooking and the baking. (See: 1st Samuel 8:11-13)

As mentioned above every thing that happened in Israel happened in Ethiopia. Soon after people rejected monarchy civil war started. The civil war was led by communist puppets. Under the leadership of the puppets, youngsters of Ethiopia were forced to join the army, the navy and airforce. Some youngsters became Generals of the army, some lieutenants, some commanders of the navy and airforce, some in charge of fifty and still some others became in charge of ten.

The rest of the population was a reserve army. Peasants in the country side were ploughing the land of the soldiers who went to the war front. They were also forced to take care of their families. In the cities and in the cities and country side ladies who had much respect in their homes were cooking food for the soldiers who had left for the campaign. From among the soldiers many who joined the army lost their lives. Intellectuals who opposed the wrong way of the government were either killed on the streets or were put into prison. There was real madness. Land lords were condemned for being rich. On the other hand supporters of the regime were shouting loud in every meeting raising high their left hands the slogan: ''Revolutionary motherland or death.'' /አብዮታዊት ዕናት አገር ወይም ሞት/. Many died. Some were eaten by vultures.

The Book of Proverbs Chapter 18:21 says: ''Words can bring death or life.'' As they said it, death came and took them away leaving some of them behind. And even those that were left behind were in total chaos. Whole country was ruined. In the midst of the chaos Christians were praying. Because they prayed they survived. Many of them now witness how God protected them at that time. This shows that it is always good to pray and to praise the Lord. Here with the Lord says:
''The sacrifice that honors me is a thankful heart.
And I, your God, will show you my power to save.''
See - [Psalm 50:23.]
This means in Amharic:
ምስጋናን፡ የሚሰዋ፡ ያከብረኛል፡፡
የዕግዚአብሔርን፡ማዳን፡ለዕርሱ፡የማሳይበት፡መንገድ፡
ከዚያ፡አለ፡፡ ምሳሌ፡ 50:23

    In times of hardship people of Ethiopia always love and encourage one another. When they love and encourage one another they become at peace. When they become peaceful, God works wonderful things. For example the devil that works against them becomes confused. This was why in 1991 the communist puppet, Mengistu ran away confused at the situation.

    The problem of Ethiopia however; has not ended yet; because there is a basic question that is asked by many from outside Ethiopia. One of these questions deals with how the relationship between the people and the government on power now looks like.

    Supporters of the government propagate that the relationship is healthy. This is an expected answer from supporters. Opponents on their behalf blame the government. This is also an expected answer from opponents. However; since the seizure of power by the new regime especially as of May 2005 election, Ethiopia is suffering from pseudo-democracy and this has been clear for every one round the world.

    We saw above the answer of opponents and supporters and the actual thing what is happening. But this has nothing to do with opponents or supporters. This is not the action of man. It is good not to blame others. This relationship only deals with God Al-mighty. If people do not confess their sins to God, life will be heavy and miserable from time to time. But when people tell their sins to God, the Lord will forgive them and then they will enjoy life and this is according to Psalm 32:1-2. So it is good to confess sins to God all the time. There is joy in confession and in forgiveness. So forgiveness and confession should be a lifestyle in order to maximize enjoyment of life.

God is full of mercy if people listen and turn to Him. In fact one of His names is God of Grace. So every body should be ready to listen to Him. He wants His people to turn to Him. When people do not listen to Him, He feels sorry. Feeling sorry, He says:" The children I rasied have turned against me." See the Book of Isaiah 1:2. God is sorry so many times. His heart is heavy with grief. Then with grieving heart, He says: "Oxen and donkeys know who owns and feeds them. But my people won't even learn." See - (Isaiah 1:3)

As we saw above God wants his people to turn to Him. So He warns people many times to turn to Him. If they do not turn, He of course punishes sinners. But there is a problem. The problem is when people are punished by God they are discouraged. When they are discouraged, they are desperate. When they are desperate He again gives them hope. When He gives hope to His people, He says:" Ask me. I will do whatever you ask me." God is better than biological father. See: John 14:13. If you also open your Bible on Hosea 11:8 you will see that God's love for His people never ends. His love for His people is strong. According to His Word, therefore; if people ask Jesus to give them freedom, He will give them freedom. He does not want His people to live under slavery or maladministration.

In Christ man is set free. In the Bible man is free. See Galatians 1:1. So taking this account of biblical truth historians say people are born free. According to the French philosopher Montesque, man in the society has equality, liberty and fraternity. This shows that historians are learning a lot from the Bible. For example historians might have learned from Moses. Then after learning from Moses historians say that the Law of Moses stands for the freedom of man. Also historians know more about Jesus. They know that He has Al-Mighty power.

Some historians teach that Jesus can set a man free. These history teachers teach that nobody is against the Lord to prevent Him from releasing man to set free. When they teach in such a way students are not only happy and would also be aware that nobody can prevent Jesus from setting man free. They say this because they know that Jesus has Al-Mighty power when governments on the earth have mighty power. Man is therefore set free in any direction. More over it is true according to the Bible the freedom that man receives from Jesus becomes real, when man has faith in Christ. Source: Galatians 5:5

Since Ethiopia is a Christian nation, this book tries to give instructions to solve problems based on the Word of God. So according to the Bible people must obey their leaders and leaders must treat their people fairly. The Lord is God of order and not confusion. So leaders must be leaders of order and not confusion if they want to imitate the image of God. God is the source of justice. So what the Lord needs from leaders is justice. On the other hand what the Lord needs from His people is to turn back to Him, confess their sin to Him and ask for His mercy. If both of them; namely leaders and subjects do not listen, the Lord has no problem. He knows what action to take, how to take it and when to take it. Take for example the people of Israel under Egyptian rule. Remember that when the Great Pharaohs of Egypt mistreated the people of God they were punished by the Lord. This is not an old history. Jesus is still alive. In the mean time people need to wait for God Al-Mighty praying, praising and worshiping God Al-Mighty. There is nothing that will solve problem except the Word of God. When people hear the Word of God and keep it in their hearts they will be blessed according to Luke 11:27-28.

There might be people who might not like to pray. It is not biblical. Rather we need to pray, because when we pray injustice will go away. Let us see one example from Book of Acts Chapter 16. Remember what happened when Paul and Silas were put into jail once upon a time.

While Paul and Silas were thrown away into a jail in one of the darkest mid-nights, they were praying and singing to God Al-Mighty. While other prisoners were listening suddenly a strong earthquake shook the jail to its foundation. Then those doors were opened, chains were broken and prisoners were released from the jail.

በመንፈቀ:ሌሊት:ግን:ጳውሎስና:ሲላስ:
ሲጸልዩ:ዕግዚአብሔርን:በዜማ:ያመሰግኑ:ነበር::
ዕስረኞቹም:ያደምጡዋቸው:ነበር::ድንገትም:
የወህኒው:መሰረት:ዕስኪናወጥ:ድረስ:ትልቅ:
የመሬት:መንቀጥቀጥ:ሆነ::
በዚያ:ጊዜም:ደጆቹ:ሁሉ:ተከፈቱ::
የሁሉም:ዕስራት:ተፈትአ::

According to Oxford Advanced Learner's Dictionary shackles are used for fastening wrists or ankles of a prisoner. Paul and Silas were fastened with shackles. But when they prayed their shackles were broken and set free. In the same token when we pray injustice will go away from the land. After that the land would be healed once and for all. This book recommends praying for the healing of the land because praying for the healing of the land is biblical and here is what the Lord says:-

''If my people will humbly pray and
Turn back to me and stop sinning,
Then I will forgive them from heaven
And make their land fertile once again. ''
Source: 2nd Chronicle 7:14

Consequently therefore when we pray sincerely, the Lord is willing to bring unity among us. So there will be unity of Amharas, Tigrians, and Oromos and with all the rest, including Eritreans. He would bring peace and prosperity for all of these people. Nothing is impossible for God. He would order the springs to gush out water as pure crystal from the valleys of the high mountains for His people, cover the mountains with fruitful vineyards, multiply the sheep, goats and cattle so that they could graze on the grassy hills so that they could produce organic mutton, beef and milk. – See Joel 3:17-18.

We saw above how God works miracles. Because our God is a miraculous God, if we obey Him, He will miraculously bless our Ethiopia. Then none from among the Ethiopians will be hungry or thirsty. All Ethiopians will be rich. How nice this is. Let us pray for that to happen.

God works miracles. But to those who do not know about miracle it is a fiction. They think that it is an exaggeration or an arrangement of tactic to show the power of God. In short for those who believe in God this is not right. God does not expect any sort of arrangement or rosy words from anybody. He has Al-Mighty power to arrange every body's life. Nobody would arrange His ways in any way.

For the Lord Al-Mighty man is less than a worm. Just for His name sake the Lord simply loves man. Because He simply loves man He arranges man's life through out the ages. So it is good to be close to God. The power of the Lord has no limit. When He sends a Word He stops injustice.

Leave alone God when a poor man becomes a close friend to a nice rich person he will get some material benefit. In the time of Emperor Haile Selassie when people were invited to the palace they were eager to hear what the Emperor would say. In the same token when one wants to pray he needs to come to God with contrite heart ready to listen to what the Lord says. One Word from God is enough. For a sincere prayer God listens and gives instruction.

Praying and staying with God is good. Praying and getting the instruction from God should not be ignored. For those who pray, God speaks. After praying it is good to be active listener and after listening from God it is good to tell the people exactly what the Lord says. This is why active prayers are needed. This is why help is wanted. On the other hand, if there are those who try to distract people from waiting the Lord, they should watch out.

God is a consuming fire. God does not like false prophets. It is good if such people back off.

The Word of God in the Bible talks to the people of God. Take for example the Word of God in – Isaiah 59:14.which says:
"Injustice is everywhere, justice seems far away.
Truth is chased out of court.
Honesty is shoved aside."

In Isaiah 59:16 God also tells us what would happen in the society. God tells us too what would happen in the last days in Matthew 24:1-14. This last day in Amharic/:"yezemen-mutach."የዘመን:መጨጨ:: This is what is happening today according to Matthew 24:1-14, not only in Ethiopia, but all over the world.

It is clear that God is always miraculous. It is clear that His miracle never ends. But what must be clear for us is that God's miracle is not history. God is always working miracles all the time. So while He talks to us we have to listen to Him. After He tells us what to do, we have to put into action what He says. If we obey the Lord even the bad days will turn good.

The Word of God says don't look to the right or to the left but trust in the Lord, so that the Lord Himself will fix all things on your behalf. In otherwords according to the Bible for those who believe in the Lord all things are possible. (See: Marks 9:23.) So what people need to know from the Bible is what God says about Ethiopia. This is what the people want at this time and it boils down to this. So people should attentively wait listening to God. There is solution from God. Otherwise; isn't every thing else about the present regime clear and known to the people and written in history? Meaning in Amharic:
"የቀረውስ:የዚህ:መንግሥት:ነገር:በህዝቡ:ዘንድ:
የታወቀ:በትእሪክ: የተጻፈ:አይደለምን?"

In the history of Ethiopia nothing has ever been secret to the general public. It is all written down. Take for example the hidden hunger of the early 1970's, which was not hidden from the general public. These days also God and people know what is being done. When the Haile Selassie regime hid the hunger at that time God was angry. So the Lord used the hidden hunger of the time to be the major cause for the failure of the regime. Thus if a leader chooses war to suppress God's people in cooperation with his cabinet members thinking he has mighty army, God would kill him over night. This is what we studied in history and what happened upon Haile Selassie. It was also due to the failure of the regime, the cabinet members, the nobles and the landlords of the time who were standing on the side of the Emperor were massacred overnight.

In Ethiopia these days it is alleged that there is severe hunger. Hunger is a state of not having enough to eat. It is lack of food. Hunger is also a strong desire for something. Whether people want to eat food or to do something, they are hungry. The People of Ethiopia are hungry for change because most are not eating enough.

When one does not eat he will have pain followed by death. So whenever; world population hears about hunger in Ethiopia their heart is like wax. Their heart melts in the midst of their bowels. Hunger is disasterous. So people need to pray for the mercy of Al-Mighty Lord with contrite heart. So that the Lord would prepare the best way for change of administration or to change the heart of the existing leaders and give them wisdom to use the resources of Ethiopia evenly and effectively, namely; fertile plains, water bodies and underground minerals would be used wisely and evenly regardless of sex, region or religion.

Pray until you touch Heaven

When you pray take a deep breathing and relax. You need to relax because you are going to be in union with God when you pray in the right way. Smiling and laughing for two or three minutes is a good therapy to get out of oneself also. What I want to tell you is to just relax and concentrate yourself on godly things and not on your things.

Begging is an art or a style of asking something from some one free of charge. When I was a small child I remember the system that beggars follow in order to get a dime from some one. I remember how they used rosy words for survival. Here I initiate no one to beg in the street using nice words, because begging in the street is not a good thing unless one has a good reason to do it. I say, it is not good because we all agree that for no good reason if a person starts to beg he will be a beggar all through out his life. We all know that, once someone starts to beg in the street he does not like to work. But we also know that he is active to beg whatever it costs him. I pick up this point because I had made a reseach when I was a young boy in the high school. According to my research begging in the street is not an easy thing. It is a tough thing to follow though.

In the same token, although; begging God to do something for you is not an easy thing, it is the right thing that a human- being needs to do when he/she lives on earth. Whether one is in problem or not there is nothing wrong with asking the mercy or the blessing of the Lord. David had done it. Jacob had done it. Moses had done it. You too, if you want to ask God some thing, do it. But when you want to beg or ask God you have to be bold in your faith in the Lord. This is the lesson from great men of prayers and that is also the main thing that makes the Lord to be happy in you. So when you sit to pray, you have to ask the Lord in faith but in respect saying:'Please...please '

But remember that when you ask God to do good for you saying 'please...please' is not enough. You have to make your flesh weak and be alert in your spirit. To be also alert in spirit you have to be weak in worldly affairs too. Besides that you need to control your tongue. So when you want to pray this is the way to be clean and come close to God. And once you start to ask the Lord in such a clean condition you should not give Him rest. You have to tell Him constantly with faith that you are desperate unless He helps you. Mere asking is not enough. You need to fast more days, sitting and praying. In the meantime you need to forget doing other business or thing. This is the time that you are in connection with the King of the universe. So you have to concentrate putting your eyes on the Lord. But you need to know that you should avoid fear because you are with the Prince of all things. So you have to enjoy and praise Him a lot.

Although this is an age of microwave God does not change in this age. One should know that style of prayer does not change through time. So you have to pray like our forefathers in humility and in the Lord's way. It is the Lord Himself who said:"Ask and ye shall receive." See John 16:23. Our ancestors were praying day and night. That was the Lord's way. They were not eatingm or drinking as they wanted. Since they were not at rest, they were not also ready to give the Lord a break. Like our ancestors you too should not let the Lord to be at rest. Thus you have to wait asking. This is a blessed time. Since it is a prayer time do not look left or right or sleep as you want. Since you are alert and not sleeping and since you are awake focus on the Lord.

Every thing has time. Discussing world affairs or talking any thing as you like at this time is not good. To discuss other things at least you must finish your prayer session. If you involve yourself in such things you might not only miss the voice of the Lord but also you will be attacked by Satan. Therefore; when you pray you should look'Godward' and nothing else. If you follow this principle you would succeed in your prayer. Otherwise you would be slamed at the face by the wicked.

It is good to learn from Jacob. One of the patriarichs of ancient Israel, Jacob struggled with God in Genesis 32:26 and became successful. You too can be successful if you pay sincerely. Unless you pay the best part of your time, energy and also quit food in order to pray and stay with the Lord your prayer might not hit the target expected.

The list of step of prayer that might help you to follow is written herewith. :

1) List down every thing you seek from God.
2) Close your door.
3) Do not curse people. If you judge people you tresspass the will of God. It is not good for you to curse. If you curse may be! You will be sick. You might even have headache. You might even develop cardiac problem or stomach-ache. The anatomy and physiology of those who curse others is not mostly normal. Those who judge others will be out of the will of God. Since you cannot bring heaven to earth when you judge stop cursing people. Also when you pray:
4) Do not support any party. Just be neutral.
5) Confess your sin
6) Confess the sin of the people on their behalf and intercede for them.
7) Pray for the leaders.
8) Pray for the hungry
9) Pray for peace.
10) Ask forgiveness of God
11) Focus on Jesus. Make your target on Jesus as a ship moves towards its sea port or as an aeroplane flies towards its airport.
12) Praise the Lord.
13) Don't talk of your needs, but talk about Jesus and his glory.

Touching the heaven is the goal of a Christian. So when one prays he should pray in spirit closing his doors and windows, turning his eyeballs onto Jesus and looking at Him and sitting under His feet. A good prayer person is attentive to hear from the Lord. He confesses, gives thanks and praises the Lord. According to Joshua 1:6-8, he reads the Bible. Day and night he meditates and thinks what the Bible says. He obeys God completely. When he prays he calls the name of Jesus with contrite heart because He is ready to help him in many dimensions of his life.

The above factors help a person who prays to be in the Spirit of God. It is when one is in spirit that he touches heaven. It is when one prays that one is able to drive the devil away. ''Pray and drive the devil away, '' says an Ethiopian pastor named Shiferaw. He also says: Press hard. Continue to pray none stop. Do not quit. Push on. Remember the more you push on with your prayer, the more your prayer will be answered. So you must ''Push.''This is because:-
P= stands for pray
U= stands for until
S= stands for something
H= stands for happens

This shows that when one prays sincerely something good will happen.

Prayer of a natural man with a carnal mind cannot move God. So when you pray for a country you live in, you should not be carnal minded. Also according to John Chapple you should be free from negativity, depression, fear, anger and stress. You should not be supporter of the poor party or the rich party. Just be neutral and pray for the peace, safety and economy of the country. Do not give your own judgement. God has a plan for His people. His plan is to bless His people with a future filled with hope and success. (Source: Jeremiah 29:11.) When praying for your country, therefore; confess your sin and the sin of the people according to Daniel 9:3-19)

Throughout the ages Ethiopia believes in the Lord. Her people seek the Lord's hand through out the ages. For example in the communist period that lasted from 1974- 1991 people were praying. As a result Communism crumbled all at once.

People of Ethiopia are Christian. They like to praise the Lord. They count a number of things what God has done for them. They praise the Lord every morning when they wake up. They praise the Lord every evening when they go to bed too. They pray day and night because Satan himself does not sleep. So Christians are busy every day. They praise daily and continuously from generation to generation because they know that God wants sweet aroma of thanks and praise from His fellow believers.

Prayer will never reach heaven, if one prays with out faith for two or three minutes. Such type of prayer does not even reach the roof of his house. So the life of such a person is sometimes up and down at other times. But the life of a person who prays prays sincerely is secured. One of the greatest prophets of God in ancient times was Daniel. His daily offering and sacrifice to God was his prayer. When Israel was in captivity, he was praying day and night. When he prayed, to express his sorrow to God, he went with out eating, dressing sackcloth, sitting down in ashes and confessing his sins earnestly to the Lord His God. (Source: - Daniel 9:3-4)

Do Ethiopians sincerely pray and fast for their country these days? Are they really showing their obedience to the Lord? Do people pray together in Churches for at least ten or five minutes? Praying is wonderful. It is also biblical. So it is good to pray for Ethiopia. No doubt! People of Ethiopia do not only pray and fast they also worship God Al-Mighty sincerely.

The Ethiopian way of expression of joy / Ellil! Ellil ellile... is widely known to the rest of the world. Though the people are worshippers they also need the finger of God. As it is a blessing to pray for Israel, it is also a blessing to pray for Ethiopia. As Israel is Promise Land of God, Ethiopia is also lovely in the eye of God. It is good to pray for America too. It is the refugee for people from all over the world. October is also a time of election. In the time before election we need to pray so that the will of the Lord for America would be fullfilled. We need to pray for America especially in the October so that the devil should be driven away from any corner of America.

When one prays for America, Ethiopia, Israel etc... God would bless him exceedingly and abundantly than a person who does not pray. Actually we live in the Last Days. In these last days it is necessary to come close to God. Working for hamburger seven days in a week drains spiritual blessings. Man does not live by bread alone. To be with Jesus is also good because He is the bread of life. To watch television is an excellent thing. But to watch it continuously steals time. Originally the word "tele" might have come from the word "to tell "and the word –"vision" might have come from the word vision or revelation and the first people who invented 'tele- vision' might have a "vision" in their mind to improve the thinking or rational power of others. So according to the dream of those who invented "television" we need to have a plan to create vision for the future.

According to Deuteronomy Chapter 30, coming closer to God is priority and this is possible through obedience. Life is a choice according to Moses. Moses said in Deuteronomy Chapter 30:" One can choose to obey the Lord. One can also choose to reject the Lord." God wants obedience because showing humility and obidience to the Lord and sincere prayer help man to bring close to the Lord and get mercy from Him. So people need to read the Word of God and turn to Him in order to get blessings.

Sincere life style and prayer is what the Lord needs from His people these days. Ancient Ethiopian people and leaders were in love of God. How about these days? Do people and leaders still altogether love God Al- Mighty? This is an open –ended question. It is not a feed back or inquiry. Obedience to the Lord is an absolute Commandment. It is very hard and impossible to pray together if people do not agree. So let us agree and unite.

Talking with God and getting instruction from God is a normal daily schedule. This is because God gives automatic answer to sincere daily prayers. If man does not pray he lags behind in making relationship with God. So if people do not pray sincerely how one is able to say that God does not answer prayer? Because God is faithful, He hears broken hearted prayer that is requested according to His Word. Take for example the prayer of Esther. She prayed for three days. God made wonderful things for the people of Israel. (See Esther 4:16.) Have you ever prayed for Ethiopia from three to five days with out food and water?

This book illustrates how prayer works in God's way. When we pray we should request God a specific question. We have to ask Him what to do for Ethiopia for example. Then when God answers for our specific prayer, we have to praise Him because we know that He answers our specific request. Specific prayer and God's answer for our specific prayer helps us to glorify the Lord. God of course knows every thing. But requesting Him specific question helps us prove that our prayer is answered by God Al-Mighty.

When we pray, we need to pray in faith. If we have faith in the Lord, we should not repeat all the time saying me...me or my.....my. We should not hold Jesus just in monopoly. He is God for anyone who believes in Him. Before we speak He knows our requests. So repeatition of the 'me or my' thing is a meaningless motive. Instead of repeating our request we need to praise the Lord. Through praising there is victory. God likes praise. He hates unbelief. Repeatition is unbelief.

To get the mercy of the Lord one has to know one thing before he prays. He must be clean and sanctified. He needs to maintain the legacy of his own identity in the right way. Take for example, the question of the history of 'birth right' in the Bible. An elder son has the right to maintain his eldership. Eldership is a right given from God for being an elder. So he should not change his God- given birth right for something unworthy. We must learn from Esau. Esau sold his birth right for a bowl of soup according to Genesis 25: 27-34. Esau and Jacob were the sons of Isaac. You can read about their history in the Book of Genesis on Chapter 25 beginning from verse 19.

These days for many people money is their bowl of soup. For Esau a small bowl of soup was to sell his birth right. As compared to birth right a bowl of soup is nothing. Had Moses loved money and power, he could have been the heir to throne of Egypt. But instead of money, he loved the people of Israel and when God saw that Moses does not care for money, but loves the people of Israel, He chose him to be the political leader, the great preacher, the great commander of the army and the liberator of the Israelites from Egyptian bondage. These days' people want power to get rich with out loving the people. When they do that, God will make their life miserable. Their nose or their total face will does not look healthy. But when they work for the general population they are lovely and what they say is lovely.

God and society expect honesty and integrity. So

one must love his fellow citizens and be honest to them. For example if a group of people; contribute some amount of money for national development but in the meantime if someone steals it, this type of person is dishonest. He sells his loyalty to a small thing. Then he loses the support of God and the people around him because he betrays his friends and in such a way he damages his history. Soon such a person would be sick from any disease. He would be sick from lung cancer and or hypertension and as result everybody would run away from him. After that nobody is going to pray for him or accompany his burial ceremony when he dies.

Satan knows lover of money. Satan does not care about integrity. So Satan initiates lover of money to steal and to lose his integrity. In order to spoil such a person Satan would show him beautiful materials. After that Satan would tell such a person to own such beautiful materials. After telling him to own these materials he also tells him to steal. After that Satan himself tells such a person that he is guilty and shameless. After that Satan himself he tells such a guilty person to feel depression. When he feels depression he also tells him to feel worthless. When he feels worthless, he tells him to kill himself. This time the thief might commit suicide. In case if such a person survives he regrets through out his life saying: '' I should have been dead when I stole that money.'' This is written for those who might steal the hungry, the homeless and the hopeless and to become rich fast for themselves. This is not prophesying but a reality. As gravity is real, this is also real. Where can such people go if there are any? They can give back the money and repent! Eating cabbage and sleeping well is good for diet, health and integrity.

Eating wild herb like wofzersh gomen /ወፍዘርሽ:ጎመን/ is better than gold or silver/ብር/ than selling personal identity or personal or spoiling national integrity. In this connection the Book of Proverb also 20:21 say:'' Getting rich quick may turn out to be a curse
''በመጀመሪያ:ፈጥኖ:የተከማቸ:ርስት:''ፍጻሜው: አይባረክም::''
ምሳሌ: 20:21.

To be honest in life is sweet. It has no complication, headache or backache. An honest man is popular wherever he goes. He does not hide himself from the public. He does not drink extravagantly. He is a free man. He walks down the streets in peace and sleeps at night slumbering until neighbors hear while he snores.

For those who are dishonest there are spies watching and checking their daily activities. From the spies of the earth one might hide himself. But from the spy of the sky; it is hardly possible to hide. So it is good to be honest everywhere. It is good for this earth and for life after death. For example; if you are a governor, it is good to be a good governor. Later you will enjoy the credit in heaven for doing well. Every thing you do is recorded and you will get a crown from God. Otherwise the Lord will throw you to hell/ the everlasting burning fire. So use the time before it expires. It is a time to work good.

When a mischivious person steals once he will appear to court several times. When he dies the spy in the sky or the angel of the Lord will wait him at the gate of heaven with his documents in his hand. From there he will take him to paradise if he has repented. If he is still a bad one he will take him to hell, the prison of God, the everlasting jail.

There is also one more thing to do. When we pray, we need to pray sincerely and according to the will of God, and not according to our will. Also if we give promise for people to pray for them, we have to pray for them sincerely. To accept prayer request and to forget praying for them is not right.

When we pray we have to close our doors and windows. We have to turn off the radio. We have to have a Bible on our side. We should not shout loud so that somebody would hear us. We need also stay for longer hours praying and fasting each day. We must stop food or drink from three to five or even more days depending on our situation. It is not biblical to spread news that we are on prayer. We are supposed to love each other. Be it in time of prayer or at other times to hate others is sin. If we are sinners God will not answer our prayers. According to Rom. Chap. 8:2 you belong to Christ and Jesus has set you free from sin and death, and because you are not a sinner God pays attention to your prayer according to Isaiah 58. That is a good thing for you.

But if you are a sinner the Lord does not pay attention to your prayer as a sinner. Also if you abuse your workers, co-workers, neighbours, friends, or family members God does n't pay attention to your prayers. Also it is good to share your food and home with the hungry. In general when we pray according to Isaiah 58 our prayers will be answered. When we live right we will be prosperous. So we need to read Isaiah Chapter 58 first when we ready to pray. Also we must trust God's limitless abilities. We nust trust Him that He will work for us. Also when we pray we must believe in the blood of Jesus, because the blood of Jesus has an overcoming power. It is written that: ''they overcome by the blood of the Lamb.'' See Rev. 12:11.

Fasting

According to John Chappel fasting is going with out food for at least 24 hours missing all three meals. John Chappel taught that there are three types of fasting when I attended Summer Camp meeting at Calvary Campground, Ayshland, Virginia in 2008 and according to her the three types of fasting are:

1) <u>Liquid fast</u>　　Water, fruit or juice and avoid soft drinks and coffee

2) <u>Total or dry fasting</u> should not be more than three days

3) <u>Partial fast</u>　A)　Missing one or two meals a day

　　　　　　　　B)　Eating only fruits and vegetables.

Source:-John Chapple ministries - Address – P.O. Box 172, Bartow, Florida 33831.

When one fasts according to Isaiah 58:6-12 he will be blessed. As thoroughly been studied by John Chappel a number of things will happen when one prays according to Isai. 58:

    1) Yokes like sickness, poverty, depression, oppression are broken.
    2) Faith increases
    3) Health increases because faith and the Spirit of the Lord cleanse the body.
    4) Anointing increases
    5) Hear the voice of God
    6) Prayer is answered ten fold quickly when fasting and prayer are combined.

According to John Chapple when we pray sincerely our soul and body will come into subjection to the Holy Spirit. Praying sincerely is the best way to comfort oneself. When our soul and body come into subjection to the Holy Spirit our flesh becomes weak and our Spirit becomes strong and it is at this time that one is comforted. When our flesh becomes weak and our Spirit strong Lord Al-Mighty / answers our prayers. This is why when we are weak in flesh we are strong in the Lord. But when we drink a lot or eat a lot or dance in night clubs we become weak in spirit but strong in flesh. In the eye of the carnal mind this is excellent. But when we see it in the Spirit of the Lord we are heading towards misery in life here on earth.

When I attended the meeting at Calvary, I had an extremely critical family problem. I was starting a brand new job in my nursing career. I was searching for a publishing company to publish this book. But giving every thing to God Al-Mighty, weakening my flesh but giving strength to my soul I passed through such a hard time with joy and success. I mention this to give you a clue how you can pass through miserable days. It is written that that God has a way through the wave meaning: /በወጁብ፡ በማዕበል፡መንገድ፡አለው፡፡/

For an individual who passes through hardship God has a way. For a country which passes through hardship God has a way too. In case of Ethiopia when a recurrence of hunger repeats and lasts long it becomes more painful to every one who hears about it. But we are not desperate. God has a way. This is why we need to pray sincerely weakening our body going out from our own box. If we pray only for ourselves we will go nowhere. But when we forget ourselves and look at the Cross, our own problem will wither away and what we pray for will be answered too. This is wisdom. Praying sincerely and seeking help from the Lord is wisdom. While we intercede for others if the agent of the wicked tries to distract us the battle is not waged by us but by the Lord.

When we request God with sincere prayer to help our country and when we make intercession for the population He gives wisdom to governors and blessings to the people. God can do any thing. Nothing is too big for Him. He can prosper the people. He can change the heart of governors to lead the population in wisdom or He might replace them completely by others. Let Him do what He wants to do. Our duty is just to be neutral and to pray with contrite heart and to accept what the Lord does and it is also good to remember that nobody can be a counselor for God Al-Mighty.

According to Charles Spurgeon, " Every wise business man periodically takes inventory of the stock of his company. He will update his accounts, examines and evaluates whether his trade is prospering or declining." This is a lesson for rulers to accomplish their part in life. So officials of a government have to search if they have public support or not. A government's account is public support. To understand this is wisdom. Any person can be rich. But a wise person seeks wisdom, because whoever is wise will win the battle. At this junction, King Solomon says:
'' The fastest runners and the greatest heroes
Do not always win races and battles
Wisdom, intelliegence, and skill don't always
Make you healthy, rich and popular?''
Ecclesiastes 9:11.

Stand Still – Exodus 14:13

You might be a lamb in the midst of wolves. In such times you be troubled and don't know what to do. In such times it is good to slow down. When you slow down you will know what to do. When you are surrounded by wolves do not look left or right. But go directly to the Lord, who is your refuge. As a bird goes to its cages you too, go to the House of the Lord. Relax. Just trust God Al-Mighty and there in the House of the Lord just woship God. There when you tell Him that your enemies are going to destroy you, He will keep you safe. To know much how the Lord keeps yo safe please read Psalm 91. In general when you follow such thing and leave everything to the Lord, He will fight for you because He says:
"Cease from anger and forsake wrath."
See Psalm 37:8
This meanse in Amharic:-
ከቁጣ፡ ራቅ፡፡
መአትንም፡ተው፡፡

To be in deep humility is good. It has credit from the Lord and from man too. When Barrack Obama runs for presidency he was deeply humble. That helped him a lot to be elected as the next president. This is a good lesson for people who want to run for election. Yelling at others in meetings and political gatherings takes nowhere. In general the credit humility in a society is beyond imagination. This is also supported by the Word of God, because the Lord says:
"The meek shall inherit the earth.
And shall delight themselves in the abundance of peace."- See Psalm-37:11.
This means in Amharic

ገሮች፡ገን፡ ምድርን፡ይወርሳሉ፡፡
በብዙ፡ሰላምም፡ድስ፡ይላቸዋል፡፡

To follow Christianity is wisdom. It has got lots of benefits. This is why a Christian should seek higher things than the worldly affairs. On the other hand unless otherwise a Christian seeks higher and better things than the unbeliever he will not be worthy in just calling himself a Christian. This shows that Christianity is a way of life and a guide for an individual. Christianity is also a way of life for the general population of a given country and the world by and large as mentioned herewith.

People learn a lot from experience. They also learn a lot from history and the Bible, the source of wisdom. History is the study of the past. People of Ethiopia since long time ago believe that a ruler on earth is an agent of God. They believe that the Lord puts a delegate on earth so that kings/ leaders should put into practice all the wishes of God. People of Ethiopia believe that a ruler protects the safety and human rights of his people in his domain.

Whether every thing is straight or not God for Him knows all of it. In this case people do not seem to have the same voice because there are different people in a society. In general innocent Ethiopian people respect their leaders and also expect good things from them. These god- fearing people just believe that their governors are wonderful and it seems that governors/ agents of God are good. But in case they are not good and do not do well; God is in charge. The innocent people of Ethiopia are now humble in front of their leaders.

The people of Ethiopia believe in the Lord. Faith develops from simple to complex. A person who has faith learns from simple things. He learns from the past. He learns from history. He waits for the future. He has patience. He is alert. He hears the voice of God. He acts hearing the voice of the Lord. A man of God does not his miserable days. He just counts what God has done for him in the past. A person who has faith stands still and sees the solution of the Lord according to Exodus 14:13. He waits for the promises of the Lord with out looking to the left or to the right. He asks God in his prayer according to the Word. Always people of Ethiopia prefer to stand still. Waiting for the promises of the Lord is scriptural. Source Ex. 14: 13   People of Ethiopia through out the ages believe that what is impossible for man is possible for God. Believing in their heart that man cannot live by bread alone but by the Word of God they just pray so that the Lord would hear them from heaven and touch their generation. This is not a simple thing. It is heavenly secret. It is also this Spiritual secret that helps them to survive.

Furthermore; people of Ethiopia seek Jesus not only for material and political aspects but also for their soul. King David was seeking God Al-Mighty for his soul. According to the scripture, King David preferred to hang around the House of God instead of enjoying the delicious food in his palace. He believed that where Jesus is, heaven is. He believed that with Jesus every thing is complte andcomfortable. This is also the principle of Charles Spurgeon who believes that Heaven and Christ is the same thing. To be with Christ is to be in heaven and to be in heaven is to be with Christ.
(See Charles Spurgeon, Morning and Evening page 46.)

So the best thing for you as a God of man is to seek God first and material things next and according to the scripture you have every thing. You are also in light. In light you are awake. Because you woke up there is no darkness for you. Through the light you see every thing as the scripture say:
''Wake up from your sleep and arise from death.
Then Christ will shine on you. ''
See -Ephesians 5:14.

Now that when people face problems it is better to give their problems to the light of the world that has a solution; namely Jesus, and sleep well overnight. It is good to look for God way. If you look for friends and act according to their advice you might not sllep well. So it is good to seek God's ways so that you can sleep well. Sleeping well in the night and staying in deep humility in the day under His feet, believing Him strongly is a great thing. He who is the judge of the universe is just all the time. Being just all the time He wipes away tears from hopeless faces. Since He is the the light of the world, He also brings for those who believe in Him more days' light high in intensity as the hours of the day steadily increases beginning from sunrise until it is mid day.

Chapter 6

Ethiopia and Tourism
Ethiopia – Peaceful for Tourists

So far you have seen the brief history of Ethiopia. Though there are internal inconveniences; Ethiopia is now peaceful for investors and tourists. It is attractive for tourists because it is a land of ancient ecclesiastical and historical sites. It is indeed a place where tourists could enjoy to the utmost visiting peaceful and wonderful sites. Besides that as a tourist one is over protected by the the government of Ethiopia and more than every thing else naturally people of Ethiopia are god-fearing and harmless. With out the presence of police in the residential areas gates and even doors of Ethiopian houses are left open in day times and even late in the evenings. A tourist would be surprised observing all this. He is safe as long as he stays in Ethiopia. He simply enjoys his visitation in peace chatting with the humble people around him and if he likes eating or drinking coffee with them. This of course would increase his joy after visiting distant sites in the afternoon scorching sun. Naturally of course coffee with others is more preferable than drinking alcohol. This is because as compared to alcohol coffee has little or no adverse effect terms in building social relationship.

Drinking CoffeeTogether

People in America spend in their spare time in starbucks. . They stay in starbucks because there is a wonderful Columbian coffee. Most starbucks also serve the wonderful Ethiopian coffee. According to Ethiopian culture home made coffee is good to spare time. As people in America enjoy drinking coffee in starbucks, traditionally people in Ethiopia also enjoy drinking coffee in their homes getting together daily with their neighbours. Drinking coffee in their homes Ethiopians exchange daily ideas and views. In doing so nobody in Ethiopia especially those who drink coffee together pass through depression in their life. So tourists when they drink coffee with the Ethiopian people, they are able to exchange ideas and views about life in Ethiopia with out being depressed. Drinking coffee in Ethiopia is in rotation, today in one home, tomorrow in the next door. As a tourist you should not necessarily be a coffee partner. If you know an Ethiopia, you just drink free of charge.

People who drink coffee are healthy. Those who drink daily might be free from diseases like diabetes and depression. The Western world is following Ethiopian style of coffee ceremony. In Ethiopia since time of immemorial neighbours drink coffee together. There is hersay evidence that these days' old people from the West spend time drinking coffee together. When they drink coffee together daily depression is gone. An Ethiopian does not drink coffee alone. In Ethiopia it is a lady that cooks the coffee. When ladies want to drink coffee they invite their neighbours to their homes so that everybody might drink together eating some snack and chatting. Anyone who wants to join the group is welcome not only to drink coffe, but also to eat the snack lying there on the table free of charge.

Finally when a tourist comes back home he will finally come back to his country saying like the prophet Isaiah how nice it is to stay with people who '' lift up their eyes on high and enjoy seeing how God created the stars (See Isai.40:26) trust in the Lord, respect strangers and wait for the Lord's mercy and miracles.

By the way the prophet Isaiah had also visited Ethiopia. When king Sargon of Assyria gave orders to cupture the city of Ashdod, the Lord told Isaiah to take of everything including his sandals from his feet. So it was at this time that Isaiah went naked and bare foot for three years in Egypt and Ethiopia.
Source: The Book of Isaih Chapter 20

Pre – historic Hominoid Sites

There are many Hominoid sites in pre-historic Ethiopia according to archaeological excavations. So as tourist you are going to visit wonderful archaeological sites. Some of them are:

1) Melka Kounture is a site 30 miles away from Addis Ababa.
2) Hadar of the Afar region in Wollo Province. This is the site where Lucy was discovered. Lucy is 3.5 million years old. The name Lucy was given her after the archeaologists listened to the music:"Lucy in the sky with diamonds.''
3) Hadar is also a site of Cholorapithicus Abyssinicus, remains of an ancient ape.
4) Dikka region – is the region where the Hominoid fossil of ''Selam'' was discovered. ''Selam'' is believed to be Lucy's baby was discovered by Zeresenay Alemseged, who was my history lecturer in Addis Ababa University in early 1980's. Source is:
Wikipedia-Encyclopedia.

Ancient Axum

Once you are a tourist in Ethiopia you have the chance to visit the ancient city of Axum. In the time of Queen Sheba the Ethiopian Empire extended from Yemen in the north to the present day Malagsy republic. This shows that Yemen was part of Ethiopia. (Sources:-1)Ethiopis by Girma Zewdie, page 14, World History by Mr. Yohannes Woldmariam, James Bruce Travels to Ethiopia Chapter 6, page 95.)

Queen Sheba's capital was Axum. In Axum there

are many remains of stelae or obelisks. Stela is a standing huge single stone shaped and molded by Axumite engineers. Axum is a historical place. It is here that the Ark of Covenant is well kept for three thousand years. Ethiopia has got a unique place in Africa studies because there are many unique things in this part of Africa. Some of the examples of the unique features of Ethiopia are the belief in the Trinity [triune] or the Sostu Silassie as it is called by Ethiopian Christians, the Tabot Christianity or (Ark of Covenant) and the Axumite civilization, the culture of eating raw meat and the culture of eating the special bread, [-engera as it is called in Ethiopia.], the unique animals the alphabets and the Ethiopian calendar.

Lasta – Lalibela

The rock-hewn Curch of Lalibela was built in the late 12th century. It was the capital city of Ethiopia after the decline of Axum. Lalibela is famous for its rock hewn Churches. When the Zaque Dynasty declined from Lalibela the capital of Ethiopia moved to Gondar. The rock-hewn Church is one of the wonders of the world.

Gondar

As a tourist the most magnificient place you visit is the seventeen century palace of Ethiopia, Gondar, which was the former capital of Ethiopia and which was the capital of Begemdir province. Now Begemmdir is called Gondar. Gondar province is located in north -eastern part of Ethiopia. The city Gondar is twenty miles north of Lake Tana. The majority of the population belongs to the Amhara tribe. The main language is Amharic. The people of Gondar believe that they speak the purest form of the Amharic language. They are also ardent followers of the Orthodox religion.

Emperor Fasildes founded the city of Gondar in

1636 as the permanent capital of Ethiopia. The city was sacked several times by outside invaders especially by the Sudanese. For example; it was destroyed by the Sudanese in the 1880's and was occupied by the Italians from 1936 to 1941. Ancient Gondar has some very good sites.

City of Fasiledes, Gondar was built in the early 17th century. In Gondar you visit Fasiledes castles. Once you are in Gondar you can also visit the Semein Mountains. In Semein Mount you find Ras Dejen one of the highest mountains in Africa. Semein Mountain is known by the United Nations for its unique birds and wild animals.

Remember that once you are in Gondar, Dabra Tabor, the city of the Era of Princes is very close to you. So you can visit Dabra Tabor and also Bahr Dar. Dabra tabor is in Gondar. It is at the border of Gojjam. Bahr Dar is in Gojjam. But they are very close to each other. Bahr Dar is a good site for tourists. Lake Tana is found in Gajjam - Bahr Dar. It is a modern city.

In Lake Tana there are many ancient Churches and monasteries to visit. Ladies are not allowed to visit some of the monasteries or Churches. To visit Lake Tana you can rent a boat. Lake Tana is the source of the Blue Nile. In Bahr Dar you can also visit the Tis –Isat Waterfalls. The Ti-Isat Waterfalls is like the Nagara Falls of Canada. The whole of this are has series of places to visit it means. So this is the area that you will enjoy at the atmost.

Addis Ababa

Addis Ababa, the capital of Ethiopia was founded in 1887 at Finfine, which is now today the sight of Filwuha or the hot spring. It became the capital of Ethiopia since 1889. Since that time, Addis Ababa became the capital of Ethiopia, It became focus of the network highways, the terminus of the railroad, which goes from Addis Ababa via Dire-Dawa to Djibouti, the site of international Airport since early 1950's the site Addis Ababa

University and the Headquarter of African Unity. People of Ethiopia in times of recruitment for job swear an oath of allegiance or loyalty in the name of the flag, which symbolizes the freedom of Ethiopia.

Things a tourist Might need to know
when looking for Hotels.

Once you are in Addis Ababa you can stay at the hotel of your choice. You can find hotels from the very cheap to the very expensive. Expensive is a relative word; though.

If one wants a cheap hotel he can get one from the regular hotels for less than $50.00 or $40.00 with a daily individual expenditure of less than $ 20.00. Taking this as basic expense one can determine also the roof of his individual expense.

On the other hand if one wants to have a place to stay him/her should make a search ahead of time and make the reservation ahead of time to stay in one of the following hotels or other hotels.

The recommendation of this paper should not be taken for granted. There is hearsay evidence that the following hotels are standardized. But the authenticity of this fact has to be counterchecked through other means. This book is not 100% reliable. Things also change through time and whosoever visits Sheraton Addis says that it is the best hotel in the country.

List of Standardized Hotels

*Sheraton Addis Five Sstars is an excellent hotel.

Hilton --Five stars is one of the best.

Ghion--- is a wonderful hotel

Ras Hotel --is a wonderful hotel

Ethiopia Hotel--- is a wonderful hotel

National Hotel--- is a wonderful hotel

Axum ---is an elegant hotel

Imperial ---is an elegant hotel

Extreme ---an elegant hotel

Lalibela ---a good hotel for a tourist

Saho ---a good hotel for a tourist

Global ---a good hotel for a tourist

Gedera ---- good hotel   for a tourist

Motera ---a good hotel for a tourist

Ararat--- a good hotel for a tourist

Yordanos--- a good hotel for a tourist

Eyerusalem--- a good hotel for a tourist

Reservation - paper work

Sim..........	Name..........
ስም.............	
Sira......	Work
ስራ.............	
Adrasha........አድራሻ.	Address..............
Edime/ዕድሜ............	Age..........
Yegebabet-ken/	Date of arrival......
የገባበት ቀን	
Metawoqiya--woreqet	Identification card
መትአወቂያ ወረቀት	
Yekiflu kutir.....	Room #..........
የክፍሉ ቁጥር	
Yesewoch bizat..	Number of people......
የሰወች ብዛት	
Yewondoch kitir	Number of male.........
የወንዶች ቁጥር	
Yesetoch-kutir...	Number of
የሴቶች ቁጥር	Female...
Zeginet...	Nationality.......
ዜግነት	
Anid kifil bicha	Only one room
አንድ ክፍል ብቻ	
Tiwilid bota...	Place of birth......
ትውልድ ቦታ	
Yemikoyubet gize	Staying time......
የሚቆዩበት ጊዜ	
Yepasport kutir...	Passport #........
የፓስፖርት ቁጥር	
Yemikoyubet mikiniyat...	Purpose of stay....
የሚቆዩበት ምክንያት	

Checking In

Tena yistilign ጤና፡ይስጥልኝ፨	May God bless you with health?
Selam! ሰላም	Let it be peace for you. Shalom!
Selam!-Lehulachihu ሰላም ለሁላችሁ	How are you all?
Sime Ato Birhanu neuw ስሜ አቶ ብርሃኑ ነው	My name is Mr. Birhanu
Ezih-kifil yizalehu ዕዚህ፡ ክፍል፡ ይዝለሁ	I have a reservation in this hotel
Kifilun-mayet echilalehu? ክፍሉን፡ማየት፡ዕችላለሁ?	Can I see the room please?
Shinit betu yet neuw? ሽንት ቤቱ የት ነው?	Where is the bathroom?
Shint-betun-mayet echilalhu? ሽንት፡ቤቱን፡ማየት፡ዕችላለቱን?	Can I see the bathroom?
Awo Tichilaleh አወ፡ትችላለህ፨	Yes, you can
Shinit betachihu nistuh neuw ሽንት፡ቤትአችጉ፡ንጹህ፡ነው፨	Your bathroom is clean.
Hotel-achihu melkam neuw. ሆትየላችሁ፡መልከም ነው፨	Your hotel is nice too.
Ahun lemegibat echilalehu? አሁን፡ለመግባት፡ ዕችላለሁ?	Yes, you Can check in
Ameseginalehu አመሰግናለሁ፨	Thank you much
Kifilu tset yale neuw? ክፍሉ፡ ጸጥ፡ ያለ ፡ነው፨	Is this hotel quiet?
Awo tset yale neuw አወ ፡ጸጥ፡ ያለ፡ ነው፨	Yes! It is quiet.
Migib betu yet neuw? ምግብ፡ቤቱ፡ የት ነው?	Where is the dinning room?

Ketemawin mayet echilalehu
ከተማውን ማየት ዕችላለሁ?   Can I see the city?

Emelesalehu   I will be back.
ዕመለሳለሁ
bhuwala ayachihualehu   See you later.
በሁዋላ አያችሁአለሁ

Site Seeing

Before / when one goes out for site seeing he/ she should know some Amharic words that deal with the landscape of the area he / she is visiting. One must also know where he / she are heading or the direction he is going and much more.

Directions

In geography we have four main directions. If you want to remember direction, think of the word NEWS, N- for north, E- for east, W- for west and S- for south. Actually the order is east, west north and south.
In Ethiopia people like to use the following words when they give direction.

East	ምስራቅ	Misrak
West	ምዕራብ	Mi'rab
North	ሰሜን	Semein
South	ደቡብ	Debub

In America people commonly use the following words when they give direction. Rarely however; might Ethiopians also use it. So it is good to know the words.

Go straight   Ketita hid/ቀጥትአ: ሂድ
Make right   Wede kegn tatef/ወደ :ቀኝ :ተአጠፍ
Make left   Wede gira tatef/ወደ :ግራ :ተአጠፍ   Make round about near the mountain Wede huwala zur ከተራራው : አጠገብ : ወደ : ሁዋላ : ዙር ::
Up the hill -Bekorebitaw- layi/በኮረብተአው :ላይ
Near the shop -Kesuku ategeb/ከሱቁ :አጠገብ

Temperature

Muket	Heat
ሙቀት	
Yekenu ayer tebay	Weather
የቀኑ አየር ጠባይ	
Kezikaza	Cool
ቀዝቃዛ	
Kezikaza bota	Cool place
ቀዝቃዛ ቦታ	
Wurich	Frost
ውርጭ	
Muk	Warm
ሙቅ	
Betam muke	Very warm
በጣም ሙቅ	
Betam betam muk	Very hot
በጣም፡በጣም ፡ሙቅ	
Betam muke bota	Warm Place
በጣም ፡ሙቅ፡ ቦታ፡፡	
Betam kezikaza bota	Very Cold Place
በጣም ፡ቀዝቃዛ፡ ቦታ፡፡	

Physical Feature

Melke'a midir/መልከአ- ምድር/	Physical Feature
Kola ቆላ	Highland
Dega ደጋ	Lowland
Yewuha botawoch የውሀ ቦትአወች	Water bodies
Erisha ዕርሻ	Farm
Meret መሬት	Land
Korebita ኮረብተአ	Hill
Zaf ዛፍ፡	Tree
Abeba አበባ	Flower
Ketema ከተማ	Urban
Lemilem bota ለምለም ቦትአ	Green area
Arenguade sar አረንጉዋዴ ሳር	Green pasture
Dingia ድንጋይ	Stone

Ashewa	Sand
አሸዋ	
Bereha	desert
በረሀ	
Chika	Mud
ጭቃ	
Woniz	River
ወንዝ	
Get'er	rural
ገጠር	
Gedel	cliff
ገደል	
Sheleko	Valley
ሸለቆ	
Hayk	Lake
ሀይቅ	
Bahir	Sea
ባሕር	
Yebahir dar	Sea shore
የባሕር ዳር	
Wossen	Border
ወሰን	
Yetefetiro habt	Natural resources
የተፈጥሮ ሀብት	
Ager-bete	country side
አገር ቤት	

Menider	village
መንደር	
Terara	mountain
ተራራ	
Meda	field
ሜዳ	
Tsehay	sun
ጸሀይ	
Chereka	moon
ጨረቃ	
Ayer	air
አ የር	
Yemenoriya akababi	Resident area
የመኖሪያ አንባቢ	
Ye-irisha bota	farm land
የዕርሻ ቦትአ	
Meda	Field
ሜዳ	
Sheleqo	Valley
ሸለቆ	
Quwatign	Rock
ቋጥኝ	
Hospital	Hospital
ሆስፒተአል	
Yemenigist irisha	government farm
የመንግስት ዕርሻ	

Site Seeing in Addis

Milikitochin manibeb
ምልክቶቹን ማንበብ

Reading at the signs

Fasiledes hotel
ፋሲለደስ ሆቴል

Fasiledes hotel.

Ye'abyssinia bank
የአቢሲኒያ ባንክ

Bank of Abyssinia

Posta bet
ፖስታ ቤት

Post office

Yetimirit minister
የትምርት ሚኒስ.

Ministry of education

Yepolis tabia
የፖሊስ ጣቢያ

Police station

Mewicha yelem
መውጫ የለም

No exit

Yaddis abeba university
የአዲስ አበባ ዩኒቨርሲቲ

University of Addis Ababa

Kennedy library
ኬኔዲ ላይብረሪ

Kennedy Library

Yetimirit faculty
የትምርት ፋኩልቲ

Faculty of education

Yeguzo wokil
የጉዞ ወኪል

Travel agency

Menilik huletegna dereja timirit bet
ምኒልክ ሁለተኛ ደረጃ ትምርት ቤት

MenilikII School

Yeamerica embassy
የአሜሪክ ኢምባሲ

Embassy of US

Jan meda
ጃን ሜዳ

Jan meda

Museum
ሙዚየም

Museum

Super market
ሱፐር ማርኬት

Supermarket

Teathre bet
ቲያትር ቤት

Theatre

Gebeya bota ገበያ ቦታ	Shopping centre
Shai bet ሻይ ቤት	Tea Room
Taxi ተአክሲ	Taxi
Mekina enakerayalen መኪና፡ ዕናከራያለን	We rent cars.

Signs in the hotels

Exit	Mewicha መውጫ
Entrance	Megibia መግቢያ
Dinning Room	Yemigib adarash የምግብ አዳራሽ
Bath Room	Shinit bet ሽንት ቤት
Hot water	Muk wuha ሙቅ ውሃ
Cold Water	Kezikaza wuha ቀዝቃዛ ውሃ
Bath-Room for Ladies	Yesetoch shinit bet የሴቶች ሽንት ቤት
Bath-Room for Men	Yewondoch shinit bet የወንዶች ሽንት ቤት
Ye conference adarash	Conference Room የኮንፈረስ አዳራሽ

When you stay in your hotel you will like the people. You will like the food, the entertainment and the culture. You will like every thing. The food is delicious, spicy and organic. How interesting and wonderful it is when you see smiling faces and disciplined employees. You might decide to stay a little bit more if you are happy.

Ethiopians love guests

The people of Ethiopia love God. They also love each other. They also love people of the ouside world. This love still continous. It never ends. It is the tradition of the people of Ethiopia to welcome all people to their homeland. Ethiopians are harmless and highly disciplined. As a visitor one can go any where in the country and be safe at any time. The soil, the atmosphere and Al-Mighty God give you warranty for peace. In general since time of immemorial Ethiopians respect foreigners. They call people coming from outside ''Ferenj.'' Ferenj means wise.

So people in all walks of life respect tourists whenever and wherever they visit Ethiopia. Besides that to keep the image of the country and to protect tourist's safety, security is alert all times. Thus beginning from the airport the safety and security of tourists is given priority.

So nondesciplined individuals can not find a loophole to do badly upon any new arrival. Besides Hotel and Tourism commission overlooks the safety and security of tourists beginning from their arrival through out their stay in the country.

Owners of hotels also help tourists when they arrive in the airport by giving free ride and tips of information about Addis Ababa. In general since ancient times because of the long history of Christian faith people of Ethiopia are very good for guests. Words like business, hotel, tourist etc.... are recent phenomena. In the past and even now Ethiopian economy was/ and still is 100% based on agriculture not on business. Before the beginning of business or before the emergence of hotel and tourism, it has been the culture of Ethiopians to love people of other lands whenever they come to their land. In the time of Mohammed for example they gave refugee to the Moslems. Pending this for a while let us deal with sight seeing.

Mount Entoto.

If you are a tourist, once you are in Addis, you might want to visit places in Addis Ababa or plan to visit places around Addis or elsewhere. Mount Entoto is very close and you can start from there.

Mount Entoto on the high mountain is a nearby place for visitation. It was a city of Ethiopia before Addis Ababa. In Mount Entoto you visit the Old Entoto's Imperial Compound and the Church of St. Mary.

Rift Valley Lakes are good resort centres. So you can make a trip to these places.

Ethiopian Culture & Religion

One of the cultures of Ethiopians is to dance calling the name of God AlMighty in Amharic, English and Geeez. One of the cultures of Ethiopians is to talk about God Al-Mighty and His triad natures. So an Ethiopia would better die if he eats with out first praying in the name of God the Father or Ab, the Son or Wold, and Holy Spirit or with out uttering the name of
አብ፡ ወልድ፡መንፈስ፡ቅዱስ

About three thousand years ago Queen Sheba gave glory to God Al Mighty. That is written in the Bible. Still what is passed on to the generations of the Ethiopians through their blood streams is the love of God. Of course we have many records how Ethiopians glorify God AlMighty after her. In the years before 1974 we know that the Abyssinian Empire and the Tewahdo Church of Ethiopia had strong unity. Though the relationship between the Church and state became loose when communist aetheists were in power the belief of the general population in God Al Mighty was growing from time to time in spite of the threat of Communists who were in power. In fact when communists tried to break the Ethiopian Christian faith revolution broke out to fight for a strong Christian faith on the soil of their ancestors. Leaders of

this revolution who rose up to survive Christianity are still alive everywhere if you want to know more. Therefore in the history of Ethiopia since 1974 there are two revolutions.
1) Revolutionary movement to over throw state leadership
2) Revolutionary Movement to spread Christianity.

The revolutionary movement that broke out to over throw millennia old state leadership had no definite goal. Until 1974 monarchy was the system of government. Unfortunately it was over thrown in 1974. The then state leadership though boasted of overthrowing monarchy, the Grand Era of Ethiopia had gone away and since 1974 Ethiopian people are going from crisis to crisis. But when you see the revolutionary movement that rose up to defend Christianity is growing at unprecedented speed that ever before.

Since 1974 Communism tried to dismiss Christianity from the surface of Ethiopia. Instead Communism itself was dismissed from the surface of Ethiopia. That was the hand of God.

It is the culture/belief /faith of Ethiopians to talk about God AlMighty and to study His Word. So since the seizure of power by the Communist regime Christianity has grown in quality and quantity than ever before the years of 1974. Until 1974 Christianity was just the state Church of Ethiopia. Today it is more than that. Ethiopian missionaries are outreaching peoples in different parts of the world. So as mentioned above travelers if they need to hear the Word of God can attend in one of the Churches of Ethiopia.

Respect of Elders

Ethiopians respect their elders. The elder of the family is highly respected by his family members and the community as a whole. Nobody can call him simply by name. He has to choose words to respect him. He has to call him Ababa,

Lietenant, major or Mr. If his name is Abera nobody should not call him Abera. You have to call him Mr. Abera, Lietenant Abera or Ababa Abera and the like. In most cases if somebody who is younger than him just calls him Abera that person is considered rude. The Amharic equivalent for rude is balege/ ባለጌ/

If an elder is coming towards a young person, the young person has to stand up when seeing the elder. If he just does not care and does not stand up to show respect he is considered a rude person/ ባለጌ/ balege. A / ባለጌ/ rude person is one who is not trained by his father or mother how to respect elders.

What has been written above portrays how fathers and mothers teach their kids how to respect elders. If the kid does not respect elders due to failure of parent negligence then the kid is called ባለጌ: ያሳደገው:: - meaning a kid deliverd and raised by a rude parent.

Injera

6000 years ago Adam and Eve were the only two people in the world which is now nearly ten billion. This is because time elapsed for 2000 years from Adam to Abraham and another 2000 years from Abraham to the coming of Jesus. The sum total before the birth of Christ was 4000 years. After the birth of Jesus we have another 2008 years and this makes the over total more 6000 years.

The world's strategic place in the world, the Middle East is:

* The 1st place for the emergence of man.
* The centre of civilization.
* The area where the three monotheistic religions of Judaism, Christianity and Islam were born
* The stragetic place for world trade.
* The centre of the world's political struggle.
* The strategic position that connects three main continents of Africa and Eurasia / Europe and Asia.

The Middle East is the area bounded by the Red Sea in the south, Black Sea in the north, Lybia in the west and the Persian Gulf in the in the east. Not far from the Middle East plants and animals were domesticated in Ethiopia between 4000B.C. and 1000 B.C. Ethiopia because of its proximity to the Middle East, Ethiopia a Christian country for the last 1700 year has been one of the few areas of the world to be inhabited by mankind. Along side with human habitation agriculure might have started in Ethiopia as early as 4000 B.C. and 1000 B.C.

በመጀመሪያ : በግስዳ : ወፍ : ጭጭ : ሳይል Meaning- in the beginning or early in the morning of human history, in other words before birds chrip or before thunder and lightening was seen in the sky /ጉርምርምተአ በሰማይ ብልጭ ሳይል/ 'Teff' the staple cereal of Ethiopian food was domesticated with in this time frame. Enset, the staple food of Guraghes, one of the tribes of Ethiopia, was also probably domesticated between 4000 B.C. and 1000 B.C.

Ever since its domestication probably for the last four or five thousand years, Teff, this tiny cereal which we use for baking injera, has been the staple food of Ethiopians. The people of Ethiopia think that every one in the world eats teff injera daily. It is surprising for them when they hear thatTeff is hardly known by the rest of the world.

A farmer ploughing

When a farmer tills his land he talks with his oxen. It seems that a farmer can communicate with his oxen. He calls them by name. He tells them to stop when it is time to stop. He appreciates them because he knows that with out them he can not grow teff, the seed used to prepare enjera the staple food of Ethiopia. The Ethiopian farmers grow teff for thouands of years.

It was only at the end of 19th century that modern schools were opened and farmers started to send their kids to schools. As time passed by farmers then learned that it is possible to get a living through education. It is possible to be a teacher in schools. It is possible be a doctor in hospitals and so on. So one of the farmers who regretted for not going to school sang a song saying:

"ዕኔ፡ በበሮቼ፡ስኮራ፡ስኮራ፡
ለካም፡በወረቀት፡ይበላል፡ዕንጀራ፡፡
ውጣ! ውረድ! በሬው! ሃ! ሃ! ሃ!

<u>Meaning:-</u>

I was boasting in my oxen.
I wonder that it is also possible to survive through writing paper (the farmer talks with his oxen when tilling theland.)

Though injera looks like a pan cake with a well cooked wott it is lovely in terms of eating food for Ethiopians. As rice is lovely for Indians, pasta for Italians, steak, burger, chicken, and pizza for Americans and Europeans, injera is good for Ethiopians.

Teff might grow in other parts of the world as wild grass. But nobody seems to give tangible evidence. So far what we know is only one thing. That is, this tiniest domesticated cereal grows only in Ethiopia. Also imagine how tiny it is. A grain of wheat might be 30 times larger than that a grain of 'Teff.'

Eating an injera with a nice wott is lovely. But cultivation of land to produce Teff is tough. It needs intensive labor. It is raely done only by one person. Cultivation of 'Teff' is great when it is done by the joint labor of a wife and a husband. While the man tills the land, the lady uproots and throws away the weeds. Throwing weeds is not a one time thing. Weeds have to be thrown away from time to time until the teff is ready for harvest

<u>Baking Injera</u>

Both the husband and the wife work together in the farm. But for cultural reason the husband does not go to the kitchen to cook wott or to bake injera in Ethiopia. Formerly from cultural point of view ladies alone do the cooking of the wott and baking of the injera. But these days from the development of modern life very few ladies are able to bake injera and cook wott because many of the ladies go to school and then to offieces. So very few ladies work in the house and cook food. Whatever; the case might be from among the ladies only experienced ladies can bake injera. All ladies can not bake injera. Process to bake injera takes a long time. Here down is the process to bake injera.

Stuffs needed for making Injera

First of all it is good to put together the tools or the supplies or the ingridients needed to bake the injera. Some of these supplies are:-

* <u>Teff -flour</u> የጤፍ ዱቄት - the most important one

* <u>Water</u> ውሃ

* <u>Bucket</u> .It is called in Ethiopia buha-iqa ቡሃ-ዕቃ

* <u>Electric or wood fire / faggots</u> –which is called magedo ማገዶ

* <u>Ground Cabbage Seed</u> which is called in Ethiopia, gomen zer - ጎመን:ዘር

* <u>A piece of rug or a piece of cloth</u>- called in Ethiopia, masesha- ማሰሻ

* <u>Cup with pouring spout,</u> -which is called in Ethiopia, mazoria – ማዞሪያ

* <u>A woman</u> -experienced in baking, traditionally called injera gagary ዕንጀራ: ጋጋሪ

Process to bake injera

In the 1st day the lady buys the teff flour. In a bucket of water she then mixes the flour and the yeast together. After that she covers the bucket tightly and leaves it at a room temperature. With in two days fermentation of the mixture takes place. Due to fermentation process bubbles are formed on the top of the mixture the bad part settles down in the bottom of the bucket. Since this part is not good for baking it is filtered slowly and thrown away. Usually on the third day the lady brings small flour and mixes it with water and boils it slightly. Then she dumps it into the bucket that contains the dough. She then mixes it thoroughly. This is called in Amharic-abisit /አብሲት::/ Waiting for half an hour or so the lady once again mixes the dough thoroughly. She then starts to take out a little bit of the mixture and putting evenly on the mitad she bakes the injera. Mital is the utensil used for baking Injera.

The lady awho bakes injera uses electric power. Before every thing else she sets the mitad ready to bake turning on the electric button. When the mitad gets warm she puts a little bit of ground cabbage/ ገሙን: ዘር/ on the mitad with a piece of cloth. Holding with her right hand the ground cabbage with a piece of cloth she presses hard on the the mitad so that it would be good for baking. After that she holds a cup to draw the dough. Then drawing some dough she pours some of it on the hot mitad. When she pours the dough she is very careful so that the dough would evenly and thinly lay down on the mitad. To do it needs an experienced lady. Laying down the thin dough and to evenly distribute it over the mitad is an art. It has to be has to be fast and perfect. Somebody who wants to do it must have a previous experience of one year or more. Otherwise it is a tough business. The lady who bakes a good injera is widely appreciated as a wonderful cook.

ሴትዮዋ፡ ትኩስ፡ ገቢረ፡ እንጀራ
ዘበበዓል፡ ኢትዮጵያ

A lady from Ethiopia baking fresh Injera or as it is called 'tikus injera' for Christmass

Food Value of Teff

There might be people who might consider teff as fodder of cattle. Of course the stalk of teff is used as fooder for cattle. In Ethiopia we call it "Chid/ or ጭድ፡/ Chid wich is a sort of hay is good cattle food. But the tiny seed of teff is a cereal. It is staple food for the people of Ethiopia.

Though food is good for the stomach, it should satisfy when eaten. For an Ethiopian eating injera gives satisfaction. Leave alone the poor, when the richest person in the Ethiopian society eats a good injera with a good wott he is satisfied. It is a good day for him because injera and wott satisfies him to the utmost than any other food.

Ethiopia has the largest number of cattle in Africa. So farmers drink fresh organic. Also teff grows only in Ethiopia. So everyone eats teff injera. Another thing that makes Ethiopia known to the outside world is the Marathon race. Ethiopia is well known in her cross country runners.

The reason why Ethiopia wins the Marathon race can be due to a number of factors. At this point the biological or hereditary affairs should not be underestimated. Eating habit is one factor. Excercise is the other. Most people in Ethiopia eat barley to generate energy. Another food that Ethiopians drink is milk. The Ethiopian 'yogurt' is called " erigo" /ዕርጎ./ When an Ethiopian drinks " erigo" /ዕርጎ/ while he eats teff injera with a good wott he is satisfied. Appart from that " erigo" /ዕርጎ/ has lots of calcium to make his bones strong. So because of these factors an Ethiopian likes to eat teff injera and to drink " Ethiopian yogurt/ዕርጎ/ with the friend he loves the most.

A person who drink's "erigo" /ዕርጎ/ daily is strong. This shows that a man in Ethiopia who drinks milk and eats barley since childhood never gets tired. Take for example the peasants of "Raya – Kobo" who have lots of cattle per head. These people are more beautiful and handsome. They grow teff for their food and sip milk for their drink. These people of Raya Azebo love to invite strangers in their homes. When the stranger wants to drink water they never give him water, but milk. These people are nice looking, tall, slender and strong. People assume that it might be due to their food and drink. Therefore; it seems but needs reearch that if people want to win in Marathon, they might need to drink milk, eat teff injera and barley and practice running.

Eating injera

Normally an Ethiopian eats three times a day and snacks in between. He eats kurse, misa and erat. These are breakfast, lunch and dinner respectively. A normal healthy person does not like to miss any of these unless he wants to fast, lose weight or is unable to eat due to personal problem. When an Ethiopian wants to eat he eats injera with meat watt, shiro watt, kitfo, tibs, and doro watt and sicy vegetables. In what ever form it is done, the staple food of Ethiopia is Injera and watt.

Also when he wants to eat food he has to wash his hands before anything else. Most foods in Ethiopia are just eaten by hand with out the use of forks or spoons. This makes washing hands is a basic hygienic care. ''Wahing hands'' has also been a global prioty health care used to prevent disease through out the ages. So one should strictly follow this procedure wherever he is or where ever he goes in his life.

In Ethiopia when one wants to eat food he has to wash his/ her hands. Food is eaten with the hand tearing the injera with fingers of the hand. Tearing the injera and wrap the watt with the injera really needs a great hygienic care. So for all of these factors washing hand is very essential in Ethiopia.

When one sits to eat, he will find the injera lay out on a wide tray or mesob on your left side and the wott is on the right side in a bowl together with a ladle to ladle out. So when one eats injera he eats one mouthful at a time. A mouthful at a time could be the size of approximately 3x3 cms wide.

Usually when you eat injera you need water. To have water available by your side enables you drink the water while you eat. If you do not like to drink water, local drinks, namely, 'tela, tej' and /or soft drinks must be available on the table. Tej or tela are home made Ethiopian beverages. In short the staple foods of Ethiopia are injera and watt and the common drinks are tej, tela and milk.

Injera the bread of Ethiopia is made from Teff flour. Tef is a unique seed only grown in Ethiopia. There are many ways to eat injera. You eat injera with Shiro watt. It is common in every house hold. Doro wott and kitfo are most favourable. The rich eat doro wott or kitfo while the poor eat shiro wott. Doro wott is made from chicken stew. It is eaten together with well cooked egg, peeled and dumped in the wott when ready.

Most people eat Siga wott almost every day. In general the Ethiopian dish consists of tibs, shiro wott, meat wott, spicy vegetable dishes and injera. Most Americans love pork. Unfortunately most Ethiopians do not serve pork. Insead most Ethiopians love Kitfo. It is prepared with special order because fresh ground beef mixed with very hot pepper called mitmita has to be marinated with nitir kibe or (well refined butter.) When people from outside hear that kitfo is prepared from raw meat they dislike it. But when they taste it they like it. For Ethiopians it is the most delicious food. And rmember that one has to give priority to his / health. Health care does not recommend it. The Bible does not recommend it. If you eat led by your private will that is your choice. But it is good not to initiate some one to eat kitfo unless it is cooked and well done.

Gursha

Gursha or Daregot - ጉርሻ/ዳረጎት: is the Ethiopian word for tip. According to Ethiopian tradition one gets gursha from a highly respected person. For example; Emperor Haile Selassie I, leader of the millennium used to give gursha/daregot for his people. In those old but good days when a person expects gursha from the Emperor he gets hectares of land or a large amount of money. Gursha in those days was a sign of care, respect and friendship. The Emperor might not remember all the people he gave gursha. But the person who gets the gursha from the Emperor remembered every thing he received from him and because of that he is loyal to the Emperor the rest of his life.

The second definition of <u>Gursha</u> slightly differs from the one mentioned above. According to Ethiopian tradition, people do not eat alone on a single small plate. Rather according to the culture every body eats from the same large plate and occasionally from the mesob, which is a product of Ethiopian handiwork. The reason why Ethiopians eat from the same mesob is to make strong their companionship and / or bond of family relationship. This is a proven fact. It does not need more explanation. When people eat from the same plate they would love each other to the utmost. For this reason all members of the family from the smallest child to the grand pa/ or grand ma eat together with a mesob every day. For an Ethiopian eating together from the same plate is very crucial.

When people eat together they express their feelings and love to each other with out reservation or qualification. They talk as they want. They also laugh from the bottom of their hearts. In the mean time they take care of each other. <u>Gursha</u> is the act of feeding your loved ones with your hand. It is the tradition of Ethiopians; before they eat they feed first their companions by hand directly by the mouth. It is not only done only once but twice, and again and again. Gursha is not only a one way process. The partner also responds in the same way and feeds his feeder. So according to the Ethiopian tradition family ties is very strong. Generally who eat together ever betray each other. Gursha or the tradition of eating together makes the bond of relationship very strong.

When the lady cooks injera, her family might be eating warm injera or tikus injera / ትኩስ ዕንጀራ/ in the dinnig room. Some times after one is satisfied he might try to stand up from his seat and move backwards. But the owner of the family also stands up and follows him to to put some injera in his mouth saying: '' in my death, please eat some more.'' In Amharic, bemotie/በሞትP: ብላልኝ፡፡ The food a man holds in his hand to feed somebody is called Gursha/ / ጉርሻ/. Sometimes it is called Daregot/ዳረጎት፡፡ It is a sort of tip. This type of culture seems to exist only in Ethiopia.

See how an Ethiopian priest feeding his friend above

The Ethiopian Calendar

Ethiopia follows the Julian Calander. The Ethiopia Calander has twelve months with thirty days each. Plus there are also five days more and this makes Ethiopia a country of thirteen months. Every fours interval Ethiopian Calander has got 366 days. The sun shines brightly every day. There is no big variation in the temperature. It is almost the same through out the year. So Ethiopia is known to the outside world as the country of thirteen months of sunshine.

Because it is a country of thirteen months of sunshine, there is no need to worry about the heating or the cooling system. It is also surprising to note that in the extra five days period, people on the premises of considering the method of counting awkward, they do not demand an increment on pay and/or rent, even if the days jump (every Leap year) to six days once in four years.

Ethiopian New Year.

The Ethiopian New year is a big holiday. It starts in September. In September it is green every where. The torrential rainfall is decreasing from day to day, though the farmers are in need of it. If there is enough rainfall in September people eat well throughout the year.

One can say a number of things about the Ethiopian Calendar. Some of which are the following.

* It is seven or eight years late than most countries in the world.
* It is thirteen months of sun shine.
* Each of the twelve months has got 30 days straight.
* The last month of the year is called Pakume.

*   Pakume is five days long. Every four years it is six days long. It is called Leap Year.

According to Ethiopian calendar Jesus, was born, two millennia ago. So it is now 2000 A.D. in Ethiopia. According to European Calendar it is now 2008A.D. But Jesus, the Word of God is Alpha & Omega

Ethiopian Calendar is unique. It has 12 hours day light and 12 hours dark night. 12 hours of sun light equals 12 hours of darkness. In Ethiopia when morning starts by 6:00 A.M. it is the end of the night darkness. After 6:00 A.M. day time with sun light starts. When day time starts you say 1 hour in the morning by 7:00 A.M. By 8:00 A.M. you say 2 hours in the morning. This is the time whereby the sun is shining and People are running to work.

So whenever you have an appointment, ask whether it is Ethiopian or European calendar. Watch out not to miss the appointment when Ethiopians count their way and you count your way. Ethiopian New Year starts in September also. Herewith are the 13 months of Ethiopia.

Months of Ethiopia

Amharic	English
Meskerem መስከረም	September
Tikimit ጥቅምት	October
Hidar ሕዳር	November
Tahsas ታህሳስ	December
Tir ጥር	January
Yekatit የከቲት	February
Megabit መጋቢት	March
Miazia ሚያዚያ	April
Ginbot ግንቦት	May
Sene ሰኔ	June
Hamle ሐምሲ	July
Nehasie ነሐሲ	August
Pagume ጳጉሚ	Pagume- is 5 days

long and it is at the end of eachyear and it is 6 dayslong every four years.

Days of the Week

Days of the Week	የሳምንቱ ቀናች
	Yesmintu kenoch
Monday	Segno
	ሰኞ
Tuesday	Maksegno
	ማክሰኞ
Wednesday	Rob
	ሮብ
Thursday	Hamus
	ሐሙስ
Friday	Arib
	ኧርብ
Saturday	Kidamie
	ቅዳሚ
Sunday	Ehud
	ዕሁድ

Chapter 7
Amharic- Ethiopian Language

Alphabet - Ethiopian Fidel

Alphabet refers to the set of written symbol. In Amharic it is called Fidel. The Word alphabet comes from two Greek words alpha and beta. Alphabet establishes a correspondence between sound and symbol.

Man naturally in his spare time likes to do something. Writing was discovered when man started to produce surplus. Writing seems pictographic originally. This began when early man became interested in drawing the picture of animals, beasts, plants and birds in the caves. Ninety nine percent of the history of man is the history of man in the caves or the history of hunters and gathers. Whenever man gets surplus he tries to do something especially when he wants to communicate with others. It might be through symbols that ancient man started to express his thoughts, to describe his interest, and to explain things found around him. Today also symbols have become a good means of communication all over the globe.

Now we have different symbols or alphabets to express ideas. Symbols are every where in the modern world. Whenever you go out of your home you observe symbols all over around you as you drive. Take a stop sign for example. If you do not pay attention for a stop sign you would suffer the consequence.

Alphabets are one of the major symbols in the world. If you do not study alphabets you will not be successful in life. Some of the major alphabets are: English, Chinese, Arabic, Latin and Ethiopian. For example in America, Amharic is one of the popular languages and in Ethiopia it is almost spoken by everybody.

Every thing we see at any time is a symbol. For example when you see a flag you think of your country, nationality and identity. When you want to get driving license, you are asked about street symbols. If you do not know those street symbols you are not allowed to drive.

In ancient Ethiopia there were various writing tools. This is because man has lived in Ethiopia since ancient times. Some of the writings were on on clay pots. Some of them were on stones. Some were on wooden blocks.

As time passed by Ethiopian scholars made simple reading and writing. This is because Ethiopian scholars had their own way of making paper, ink and pen. Writing in Amharic is simple. Once you start to write and read in in Amharic you will get a lot of hidden ancient treasure, and that is knowledge.

Ethiopia used to make paper out of sheep and goat's skin. Paper made out sheep and goat's skin is called parchment. It is called 'Birana' in Amharic. When Birana is made, one side of the leather is scraped smooth. It was on this smooth scraped surface/ birana / that Chronicles of kings, the Bible and other historical accounts were written and ancient pictures drawn. Ethiopia priests were experts in making different kinds of ink out of different types of leaves and other things mixing and boiling together. The dominant colors of the ink were red and black. In such a way that Ethiopian writing/paleography/developed since time of immemorial and this is what helped to preserve the Bible, the Ethiopian culture, the secular and the Church history/and or Tabot Christianity. One of the great heritages of Ethiopian civilization is her development of alphabets. Ethiopian writing is simple if you study the alphabets 1st. To write in English you need to know the spelling of each word. This is life long ting. Herewith is a table that shows English alphabets and Amharic fidel.

The table shows the basic difference between the English vowels and the
Ethiopian Alphabets in a simplified way.
Amharic has no small or capital letters while each Amharic letter has seven orders.
 Example
አ   ኡ   ኢ   ኣ   ኤ   -   ኦ

The following table shows how we use the English Alphabets from A –Z in relations with Amharic alphabets

English Alphabets Capital Letter	small letter	Amharic alphabets	
A	a	አ	ART
B	b	በ	Bird
C	c	ከ	Cut
D	d	ደ	Dirt
E	e	ኤ	End
F	f	ፈ	First
G	g	ገ	Girl
H	h	ሀ	Hand
I	i	ኢ	India
J	j	ጀ	Just
K	k	ከ	cut
L	l	ለ	London
M	m	መ	Must
N	n	ነ	Nun
O	o	ኦ	Okay
P	p	ፐ	Purple
Q	q	ኩ	Quote
R	r	ረ	Rust
S	s	ሰ	Sun
T	t	ተ	turn

One Ton=10 quintals. 1 quintal =220 lbs.

U	u	ኡ	Ur - birth place of Abraham
V	v	ñ	Verb
W	w	ወ	War
X	x	አክስ	X-hromosome
Y	y	የ	Yes
Z	z	ዝ	

Z is the 26th letter of the English alphabet

When we want to write in the English we use letters to form words; whereas when we want to write in Amharic we use 'fidel.' This shows that a <u>Fidel</u> in Amharic is equivalent to a letter in English. A person who wants to write in English studies spelling throughout his life; whereas a person who writes in Amharic studies 'fidel' once in his life. There is a big difference between once in life and through out in life. Because of this it is good to urge Ethiopian children to study Ethiopian letters just once in their life time. The purpose of writing this book is initiate Ethiopian kids study ''Fidel'' and to preserve the history of their mother land. Studying English is wonderful. It is not only the medium of communication in the world but is also a business language. Amharic which has been used for centuries in the ''Horn'' is now only a major official language of Ethiopia. English is spoken all over the world twenty four –seven.

Amharic Alphabets

In the Ethiopian language (አ) is like (A) in Latin. (አ) in Ethiopia is the only vowel though it is divided into seven orders. (አ) and its seven orders give readable sound to all consonants. Because of (አ) you do not need to study spelling through out your life. (አ) and its seven orders make a magnificent contribution in reading and writing. The secret of application (አ) of and its seven orders is the secret of an easy method to study Amharic. Example for 'A' can be ''An''
Here is (አ) that is A, the Ethiopian vowel with its seven orders.
አ   ኡ   ኢ   ኣ   ኤ   -   ኦ

አ is pronounced as 'A. 'Example America
ኡ is pronounced as '' U''. Take the letter P for example.
P is just P. If you write P and U together it will be 'PU' and add T. It becomes 'PUT'. It makes sense.
At other times 'OO' can be read as 'U'.
Example: - Moon, Spoon.

ኢ- I- pronounced as igloo, dig, bit etc…
አ-A- pronounced as art, bar, man…
ኤ-E-pronounced as hell, men, sell…
- -E- pronounced as chicken, sudden, lived…
ኦ-O- pronounced as ostrich, octopus, orange…

Ethiopian consonants

ሀ-is like HA- example hand.
ሉ-is like LU- example lung,
ሙ -is like MU- example muscle, muggy, must…
ሱ-is like SU- example sun.
ሩ -is like RU- example rust, run…
ሹ-is like SHU- example shuttle…
ቀ is like qu—example
ቡ-is like BU- example burn, burst…
ቱ-is like TU- example turn
ቹ-is like CHU- example church…
ኑ-is like NU- example nurse…
ኙ-is like GNU
ኩ-is like CU- example curse…
ወ-is like WO- example word, won
ዘ-is like ZE .Zebra starts with Z
ዠ-is like ZH- example measure…
የ-is like YE- example yes, yet…
ዱ-is like Du- example dull, dust…
ጁ-is like JU- example just…
ጉ-is like Gu- example gum…
ፉ-is like FU- example fun…
ፑ-is like PU- example purse…
ቨ-is like VE- example verb…

      Ethiopia has some more alphabets, which are difficult for people whose first language is English. These alphabets are the following.

ቀ-is pronounced like Ke'
ጨ- is pronounced like Che'
ጸ- is pronounced like Tse'

ﬀ- is pronounced like Te'
Ethiopia has also some more alphabets, which look like the following.

ቄ	is like K'UA
ቍ	is like K'WU
ቊ	is like K'UI
ቃ	is like K'UA
ቄ	is like K'UE
ቅ	is like 'KE'
ቆ	is like KUO
ሏ	is like LWA
ሯ	is like RWA
ሿ	is like SHWA
ኳ	is like K'WA
ሟ	is like MWA
ሷ	is like SWA
ቧ	is like BWA
--	is like TWA
--	is like TC'WA
ጿ	is like TS'WA

Writing Ethiopian Alphabets

       The first letter in Ethiopia is (G) and is written like {HA.} The next letter is (K) and is written like {LE}. In the following pages you will see the letters written in order. Actually there are seven orders.

       The three 'R' method of learning is the best way of study. These are reading writing and reciting. Herewith I want you to write the following Ethiopian Alphabets.

The First orders of the Ethiopian alphabets are herewith:-

ሀ ለ ሐ መ ሠ ረ ሰ ሸ ቀ በ
ተ ቸ ኀ ነ ኘ አ ከ ወ ዐ ዘ ዠ
የ ደ ጀ ገ ጠ ጨ ጰ ጸ ፈ T

Vowels

Vowels - A, E, I, O, U & Y

H	ሀ	ሁ	ሂ	ሃ	ሄ	ህ	ሆ
L	ለ	ሉ	ሊ	ላ	ሌ	ል	ሎ
H	ሐ	ሑ	ሒ	ሓ	ሔ	ሕ	ሖ
M	መ	ሙ	ሚ	ማ	ሜ	ም	ሞ
S	ሠ	ሡ	ሢ	ሣ	ሤ	ሥ	ሦ
R	ረ	ሩ	ሪ	ራ	ሬ	ር	ሮ
S	ሰ	ሱ	ሲ	ሳ	ሴ	ስ	ሶ
Sh	ሸ	ሹ	ሺ	ሻ	ሼ	ሽ	ሾ
Q	ቀ	ቁ	ቂ	ቃ	ቄ	ቅ	ቆ
B	በ	ቡ	ቢ	ባ	ቤ	ብ	ቦ
T	ተ	ቱ	ቲ	--	ቴ	ት	ቶ
C	ቸ	ቹ	ቺ	ቻ	ቼ	ች	ቾ
H	ኀ	ኁ	ኂ	ኃ	ኄ	ኅ	ኆ
N	ነ	ኑ	ኒ	ና	ኔ	ን	ኖ
Gn	ኘ	ኙ	ኚ	ኛ	ኜ	ኝ	ኞ
A	አ	ኡ	ኢ	ኣ	ኤ	--	ኦ
Ke	ከ	ኩ	ኪ	ካ	ኬ	ክ	ኮ
H	ኸ	ኹ	ኺ	ኻ	ኼ	ኽ	ኾ
W	ወ	ዉ	ዊ	ዋ	ዌ	ው	--
A	ዐ	ዑ	ዒ	ዓ	ዔ	ዕ	ዖ
Z	ዘ	ዙ	ዚ	ዛ	ዜ	ዝ	ዞ
G	ገ	ጉ	ጊ	ጋ	ጌ	ግ	ጎ
T	ጠ	ጡ	ጢ	ጣ	ጤ	ጥ	ጦ
Ch	ጨ	ጩ	ጪ	ጫ	ጬ	ጭ	ጮ
P	ጰ	ጱ	ጲ	ጳ	ጴ	ጵ	ጶ
S	ጸ	ጹ	ጺ	ጻ	ጼ	ጽ	ጾ
S	ፀ	ፁ	ፂ	ፃ	ፄ	ፅ	ፆ
F	ፈ	ፉ	ፊ	ፋ	ፌ	ፍ	ፎ
P	ፐ	ፑ	ፒ	ፓ	ፔ	ፕ	ፖ

Expanded forms or the seven orders of the Amharic alphabets follow. In the open space provided I urge you to please practice to copy looking the letters written on the left hand side.

Write/ read/ recite/ ጻፍ/አንብብ/በቃልህ አጥናው፡፡

Write-read-recite *መጻፍ/ማንበብ/በቃልህ አጥናው*፡፡

Phonetics

Phonetics: - is a branch of Linguistics dealing with the perception of speech sounds. In order to vocalize a speaker must construct his air flow at same point in the delivery using either the tongue or mouth or throat. Articulator phonetics is shown here below divided into two organs, namely:

1) <u>Movable organs</u>: are such organs like lips, jaws, tongue, vocal chords etc…

2) <u>Stationary organs</u>: are organs like teeth.

Ethiopian Vowels & Consonants

In Ethiopia we have many consonants. Almost 99% of the letters are consonants. But we have only on vowel. It is synonymous with the Latin letter A. it is shaded with black here below. The rest of the letters under it are its seven orders.

ከ

ከ a............................
ኩ u............................
ኪ I............................
ካ a............................
ኬ ıe...........................
-- e............................
ኮ O............................

Numbers of Ethiopia

Number is defined in Oxford Learners' Dictionary as followed:
<u>Number</u>: is an idea, a symbol or word indicating a quality of units. Number is abbreviated as No. or no. In U.S it is symbolized as #.
<u>Numeral</u>: is a symbol representing a number. Example:- Arabic, Roman, Ethiopian Herewith we have Arabic, Ethiopian, and Roman Numbers.

Arabic	Roman	Ethiopian
0	--	--
1	I	፩
2	II	፪
3	III	፫
4	IIII or IV	፬

5	V	
6	VI	
7	VII	
8	VIII	
9	VIIII or IX	
10	X	
11	XI	
12	XII	
13	XIII	
14	XIIII	
15	XV	
16	XVI	
17	XVII	
18	XVIII	
19	XIIII or XIX	
20	XX	
21	XXI	
22	XXII	
23	XXIII	
24	XXIV or XXIIII	
25	XXV	
26	XXVI	
27	XXVII	
28	XXVIII	
29	XXIX	
30	XXX	
31	XXXI	
32	XXXII	
33	XXXIII	
34	XXXIV	
35	XXXV	
36	XXXVI	
37	XXXVII	
38	XXXVIII	
39	XXXIX	
40	XL or XXXX	
41	XLI	

42	XLII	፵፪
43	XLIII	፵፫
44	XLIV	፵፬
45	XLV	፵፭
46	XLVI	፵፮
47	XLVII	፵፯
48	XLVIII	፵፰
49	XLIX	፵፱
50	L	፶
51	LI	፶፩
52	LII	፶፪
53	LIII	፶፫
54	LIV	፶፬
55	LV	፶፭
56	LVI	፶፮
57	LVII	፶፯
58	LVIII	፶፰
59	LIX	፶፱
60	LX	፷
61	LXI	፷፩
62	LXII	፷፪
63	LXIII	፷፫
64	LXIV	፷፬
65	LXV	፷፭
66	LXVI	፷፮
67	LXVII	፷፯
68	LXVII	፷፰
69	LXIX	፷፱
70	LXX	፸
71	LXXI	፸፩
72	LXXII	፸፪
73	LXXIII	፸፫
74	LXXIV	፸፬
75	LXXV	፸፭
76	LXXVI	፸፮
77	LXXVII	፸፯
78	LXXVIII	፸፰

79	LXXIX	፸፱
80	LXXX	፹
81	LXXXI	፹፩
82	LXXXII	፹፪
83	LXXXIII	፹፫
84	LXXXIV	፹፬
85	LXXXV	፹፭
86	LXXXVI	፹፮
87	LXXXVII	፹፯
88	LXXXVIII	፹፰
89	LXXXIX	፹፱
90	LXXXX or XC	፺
91	XCI	፺፩
92	XCII	፺፪
93	XCIII	፺፫
94	XCIV	፺፬
95	XCV	፺፭
96	XCVI	፺፮
97	XCVII	፺፯
98	XCVIII	፺፰
99	XCIX	፺፱
100	C	፻
200	CC	፪፻
300	CCC	፫፻
400	CCCC or CD	፬፻
500	D	፭፻
600	DC	፮፻
700	DCC	፯፻
800	DCCC	፰፻
900	CM	፱፻
1000	M	፻፻
2000	MM	፪፻፻
3000	MMM	፫፻፻

Roman and Ethiopian numbers have no the number zero. Zero is written as (0) in English. It is only Arabic number which has got the number zero (0). Ethiopian and Roman numbers have no fraction or decimal. So we use Arabic numbers in mathematics, algebra and geometry.

፩	አንድ Anid	One	1
፪	ሁለት Hulet	Two	2
፫	ሶስት Sosit	Three	3
፬	አራት Arat	Four	4
፭	አምስት Amisit	Five	5
፮	ስድስት Sidist	Six	6
፯	ሰባት Sebat	Seven	7
፰	ስምንት Simint	Eight	8
፱	ዘጠኝ Zetegn	Nine	9
፲	አስር Asir	Ten	10

፲፩	አሥራ አንድ Asira Anid	Eleven	11
፲፪	አሥራ ሁለት Asira hulet	Twelve	12
፲፫	አሥራ ሦስት Asira soste	Thirteen	13
፲፬	አሥራ አራት Asira arat	fourteen	14
፲፭	አሥራ ምስት Asira amist	fifteen	15
፲፮	አሥራ ስድስት Asira sadist	sixteen	16
፲፯	አሥራ ሰባት Asira sebat	seventeen	17
፲፰	አሥራ ስምንት Asira simint	eighteen	18
፲፱	አሥራ ዘጠኝ Asira Zetegn	nineteen	19
፳	ሀያ Haya	twenty	20
፴	ሰላሳ Selasa	thirty	30
፵	አርባ Ariba	forty	40

፶	አምሳ Amisa	fifty	50
፷	ስልሳ Silsa	sixty	60
፸	ሰባ Seba	seventy	70
፹	ሰማኒያ Semaniya	eighty	80
፺	ዘጠና Zetena	ninety	90
፻	መቶ Meto	one hundred	100
፼	ሺ Shi	one thousand	1000

Language

Language is for communication. There is no any other creature on the surface of the earth that can communicate with one another except man. This is because God created man in His own image and likeness, and God always communicates with His creatures in one way or another.

First of all one should know that the only God that can speak is God Al-Mighty. By His power of command and communication everything is created according to Genesis Chapter one. Then man who is created in the image and likeness of God is able to communicate because God has given man wisdom and voice. Through the voice man is able to make a language and this is what is called speech.

So the reason why God gave man the power to

make voice is to enable him to speak and through his voice to praise and worship God Al-Mighty and this is an endless process. This is the desire of God. Worship never stops.

Circumstances should not or would not limit man to praise His God, because in the Book of Joshua especially on Chapter 1:8 God Himself says:...meditate this book day and night .....For then you will make your way prosperous, and then you will have success.

In the mean time if people use their voice for their own success, God will not be interested according to the story of the '' Tower of Babel.'' You can read it in the Book of Genesis Chapter Eleven.

But if people use their voices to praise and worship the Lord they are doing according to the will of God. For example take the story of Paul and Silas in the Book of Acts on Chapter 16:25. Here is the story. Paul and Silas were put in jail. But by mid night Paul and Silas were praying and singing and singing praises to God, while other prisoners listened. Suddenly a strong earthquake shook the jail to its foundations. The doors opened and the chains fell from all the prisoners. This shows that gives us voice so that we should praise Him and worship Him. In the world we live in we need wisdom to know and to do.

Every thing we do in this world has a formula and a reason. So you need to know the formula and the reason. If you know the formula and the reason why we do we will have access to learn more. For a student in particular with out learning a little bit about this if he just goes back and forth from school to his home and from his home to school he will achieve little in his endovear.

God has perfectly created the anatomy of man in order to help man to do what he wants. For example to listen to voices God has given man two ears. To speak out the voices God has given man one mouth. This shows that listening takes twice as much as speaking. This shows that listening carefully is very important before making speechs and again this is the treason God created different anatomical parts. And you should be active listner and slow to speak.

When I planned to write this book I try to portray the glory of God, because I believe in the capacity God gives, we should in return try to give glory to the creator of the universe. So in this book why I quoted verses from the Bible is to glorify God.

Ethiopian alphabets and phonetics

There is no an easy thing in the world we live in. Every thing needs some type of effort, plan and labor. For example for a good student to be successful he should have a good command of language. This is to show that if one needs to be a good student he/ she should know key factors that make his/ her aspiration for education successful. Studying spellings of words and phonetics are key factors to have a good command of language. Professor Baye and I were classmates when we were attending class in twelveth grade in Prince Bede Mariam Demonstrative School in Addis Ababa. What I share for you now is what Baye explained to me. He was good in this and later he became professor of Linguistics later.

Phonetics is a branch of linguistics dealing with physical nature and perception of speech sounds. To make words/ or vocalize / the speaker must construct air flow at some point using his tongue, mouth or throat. Here below articulator phonetics is shown. Organs of articulation are divided into 1) Movable Organs 2) Stationary Organs.

Movable organs are organs like lips, jaws, tongue, or vocal chords. Stationary organs are organs like teeth. So to learn a certain language one needs to know about Phonetics. He needs to know about vowels and consonants. In Amharic we have vowels and consonants. In the English language there are vowels and Consonants too. In Amharic the vowel is Anababi/ አናባቢ/ and Consonant is/ Tenababi /ተናባቢ/

In Amharic (አ) is a vowel. So it performs the work of the vowel. In English vowels are: - A - - E- - I - - O - - U and - - Y-. Vowels are five in number. Sometimes Y is also used as

vowel. When – Y - is included they are six in number. So in English we have many vowels. However; (-Y-) is also used as a Consonant. When it is used as a consonant it is written at the beginning of a word. For example, take the word
"You" where the beginning of the word 'You' is 'Y.'
In Amharic we have only one vowel. The Amharic vowel is the letter (አ). However; አ has got seven orders. These are:

አ   ኡ   ኢ   አ   ኤ   --   ኦ

In Amharic the alphabet (አ) is equivalent to the English alphabet (A.) This is when we talk about phonetics. In language study one should give attention to sounds of alphabets and words. In this case one should give attention to the spelling that represents the sounds of words or letters or alphabets.

Every time when one studies a certain language, he should pay attention to phonetics. Originally phonetics was a Greek word, " Phone," meaning, "sound or voice."

አ   ኡ   ኢ   አ   ኤ   --   ኦ
A   U   I//E/Y A   E   O

As you know when you go to any medical dictionary like Taber's Cyclopedic Medical Dictionary or Mosby's Medical & Nursing Dictionary or to Oxford Advanced Learner's dictionary or to any ordinary dictionaries you see that vowel A is used sometimes like 1) አ sometimes like 2) ኤ , sometimes like 3) ዓ and sometimes like 4) ኦ this shows that from dictionaries you see not only meanings but also spellings and much more.

Since you are familiar with English you know that when you read dictionaries it is good to read appropriately, learn attentively and observe analytically.

So from what I read, learn and observe a little bit from dictionaries I have presented to you a guide line to learn Amharic. When a person teaches he has to start from simple and then go on to complex. Already you know English. That is simple for you. But Amharic is complex to you now. But as you study a little bit every day you will be able to communicate speaking in

Amharic as the saying goes on: "One mouthful at a time finishes an elephant."
 The other thing that will help you study a language is the love and respect you give to the people. So if you love the people and respect their cultures and over all their identities you will accept them as they are. This then will eventually help you to study their language very easily, this case Amharic in a short time.
 One cannot exhaust learning every thing in a dictionary. I have learned only a little bit. For example one might learn that there are many words in the dictionary that have the following endings.

Noun ስም

Noun is a word. It is used to name a person, place or thing. ስም ቃል ነው፡፡ የሚጠቅመውም ስምን ቦትአንና ነገርን ለመጥራት ነው
Here are examples. ዕነዚህ ምሳሌዎች ናቸው
(Person)- Bruce, James - ሰው- ብሩስ ጄምስ
<u>Example</u>- Place – museum, city, Ethiopia – ምሳሌ ---ቦትአ- ሙዚያም- ከተማ- ኢትዮጵያ
<u>Thing</u> – Example- , cow, dog
<u>ነገር-</u> ምሳሌ ላም - ውሻ

Pronouns/ተውላጠ -ስሞች

Pronouns are divided as 1st Person, 2nd Person and 3rd Person
ተውላጠ ስም -1ኛ መደብ 2ኛመደብ ዕና 3ኛ መደብ ተብሎ ይከፈላል
First person- in English and in Amharic
አንደኛ መደብ
First person - is divided into – singular and plural.
አንደኛ መደብ፡ ነጠላና፡ ብዙ፡፡ተብሎ፡ ይከፈላል፡፡
Second person- is divided into singular and plural.
ሁለተኛ ፡መደብ፡ ነጠላና ፡ ብዙ፡ ተብሎ፡ ይከፈላል፡፡

Third Person – is divided into singular and plural
ሶስተኛ መደብ፡ ነጠላና ፡ ብዙ፡ ተብሎ፡ ይከፈላል፡፡
First person refers to the person speaking.
እንደኛ መደብ- የሚናገረውን ሰው ይመለክተአል
Second person – is the person spoken to.
ሁለተኛ መደብ - የምትናገረውን ሰው ይመለክተአል
Third person – refers to the person spoken about.
ሶስተኛ መደብ ስለሚነገርለት ሰው ይመለክተአል
First Person Singular- **እንደኛ መደብ በነጠላ ቁጥር**
Examples- of first Person Singular – I, Me, My
ምሳሌ -- እንደኛ መደብ- ዕኔ- ዕኔን- የኔ
Examples- of first Person Plural – we, us, our, ours
ምሳሌ እንደኛ መደብ ብዙ ቁጥር- ዕኛ - የኛ - ዕኛን
Examples- of second Singular – you, your, yours
ሁለተኛ መደብ በነጠላ ቁጥር አንተ የአንተ የአንተን
Examples- of second Person Plural
you, your, yours
ምሳሌ ሁለተኛ መደብ በብዙ ቁጥር
ዕናንተ- የዕናንተ- ዕናንተን
Third Person Singular –he, him, his, she, her, hers, It, its
ምሳሌ ሶስተኛ መደብ በነጠላ ቁጥር- ዕርሱ- ዕርስዋ- የዕርሱ- ዕርሱ-
Examples- of Third Person Singular – he, she it
ምሳሌ - ሶስተኛ መደብ፡ ነጠላ፡፡ ዕርሱ፡ዕርስዋ፡ ዕርሱ/ ለዕቃ/
Third Person Plural- they, them, theirs
ምሳሌ - ሶስተኛ መደብ ብዙ ቁጥር -ዕነርሱ -ዕነርሱን- የዕነርሱ

አንደኛ መደብ

ነጠላ	ብዙ
ዕኔ	ዕኛ

ሁለተኛ መደብ

ነጠላ	ብዙ
ለወንድ አንተ	ዕናንተ
አንቺ	ዕናንተ
አንተ	ዕናንተ
አንቺ	ዕናንተ

ሶስተኛ መደብ

ነጠላ	ብዙ
ዕርሱ	ዕነርሱ
ዕርስዋ	ዕነርሱ
ለወንድ ዕርሱ	ዕነሱ
ለሴት ዕርስዋ	ዕነሱ

Body Language
Greetings

Greeting is an art in Ethiopia. Ethiopians can communicate with the use of their body parts with out the use of language. They have the know-how to communicate with out the use of words effectively. When one person meets with another person one can observe the movement of the body to greet and the repetition of the same word over and over going between the two parties. Usually there is repetition of words or sentences when two or more persons communicate and when they have no secrets. There is no movement of mouth and no words when the thing is secret.

Culturally while one meets another person on his way and if one is on a horse back he stops ridding. Then he stands on the ground to bow down and show his respect. This is not only in Ethiopia. Such type of body language is common in the rest of the world.

Feminine Difference in Amharic

In Ethiopia there is also feminine and male difference in Conversation. In English conversation regardless of who you are people greet you saying: - "How are you?" But Ethiopians consider the male / female aspect.

English	Amharic	Amharic
Male	Wende	ወንድ
Mr.	Ato	አቶ ያገባ
Mr.	Ato	አቶ ያላገባ
How are you?	dehnaneh?	ዕንዴት ነህ?
What is your name?	simih manew?	ስምህ፡ማን ነው?
Female	Seit	ሴት
Miss	Wezerit	ወይዘሪት ያላገባች
Mrs.	Woizero	ያገባች
How are you?	denanesh?	ደህና ነሽ?
What is your name	Simish-manew?	ስምሽ፡ ማነው?

Noun is name of things. A noun can be singular. A noun can also be plural. Example cow (cows). Here you have added the letter 'S' at the end. In English you can also add 'IES'. Example candy (candies.) Sometimes you may also add 'ES', example hero (heroes).

In Amharic simply add "woch." to form the plural form of a noun.

Amharic	Amharic	English
netela ነጠላ	Bizu ብዙ	singular
Lam ላም	Lamwoch ላሞች	cow
Keremila ከረሜላ	Keremilawoch ከረሜላዎች	candy
Jegina ጀግና	Jeginawoch ጀግናዎች	Brave hero
Seit ሴት	Seitwoch ሴቶች	woman
Ketema ከተማ	Ketemawoch ከተማዎች	city
Semay ሰማይ	Semayat ሰማያት	sky
Kulf ቁልፍ	Kulfwoch ቁልፎች	Key
Wusha ውሻ	Wushawoch ውሾች	dog

Pronoun	ተውላጠ ስም
(I... We....	እኔ እኛ
You..You..	አንተ አንቺ እናንተ
He......She....	እሱ እስዋ
It...	እሱ (ለእቃ)
They...)	እነሱ

Questions ጥያቄዎች

Fill up the following blank Spaces in Amharic
የሚከተሉትን ባዶ ቦታእወች በአማርኛ ክፍቱን
ቦትእ ሙላ

English	English	Amharic	Amharic meaning
1st person	I	Enie	1-----;---
1st person- plural.	We	Egna	2-----;---
Singular 2nd person- Male	You	Ante	3----;------
Female singular	You	Anchi	4.-----;----
Plural 2nd person	You	Enante	5------;----
3rd person Male	He	Esu	6------;----
3rd person F	She	Esua	7-----;-----
3rd person - thing	It	Esu for a thing	8------;----
3erd.--Person	They	Enesu	9-----;-----

Answers to the questions are given here below.
ለጥያቄወቹ መልስ ከዚህ ቦትእች ተሰጥቶአል

1.	እኔ	5.	እናንተ
2.	እኛ	6.	እሱ
3	አንተ	7.	እሷ
4	አንቺ	8.	እሱ ለእቃ
		9.	እነሱ

Possessive Pronouns

My, mine, our, ours, your, yours, his, her, hers, its

English	Amharic	Amharic
My	Yenie	የኔ
Mine	Yenie	የኔ
Our	Yegna	የኛ
Ours	Yegna	የኛ
Your	Yante	ያንተ
Yours	Yante	ያንተ
His	Yesu	የሱ
Her	Yesua	የስዋ
Hers	Yesua	የስዋ
Their	Yenesu	የነሱ
Theirs	Yenesu	የነሱ
It's – for a thing	Yesu	የሱ

Amharic	Amharic	English
Anid	አንድ	one
Huletum	ሁለቱም	both
Eyandandu	ዕያንዳንዱ	each
Minim	ምንም	none
Bizu	ብዙ	Many-countable
Bizu	ብዙ	Much uncountable
Hulu	ሁሉ	All

Amharic	Amharic	English
Anid bir	አንድ ብር	One dollar
Hulet sewoch	ሁለቱ ሰዎች	Both men

Huletachihu	ሁለትአችሁ	Both of you
Huletachin	ሁለትአችን	Both of us
Bizu touristoch	ብዙ ቱሪስቶች	Many tourists
Bizu genzeb	ገንዘብ ብዙ	Much money

Amharic	Amharic	English
Awo	አወ	yes
Yelem	የለም	no
Awo esu neuw	አወ፡ዕሱ ነው፡፡	Yes, he is
Awo esu neuw	አወ፡ዕሱ ነው፡፡ (ለዕቃ)	Yes, it is
Awo enie negn	አወ፡ ዕኔ ነኝ፡፡	Yes, I am
Awo ante neh	አወ፡አንተ ነህ፡፡	Yes, you are.
Yelem ante adelehim	የለም፡ አንተ አይደለህም፡፡	No, you are not.
Yelem esu adelehim (for a thing)	የለም፡፡ዕሱ አይደለም (ለዕቃ)	No, it is not.

መቻል	mechal	can
ዕኔ ዕችላለሁ	Enie echilalehu	I can
አንተ ትቸላለህ	Ante tichilaleh	You can
ዕኔ አልችልም	enie alchilim	I can not
ዕኛ አንችልም	egna anchilim	We can not

ዕሱ አይችልም	Esu ayichilim	He can not
ዕኔ፡መምጣት አልችልም	enie memitat alchilim	I can not come
ዕኔ፡ መሄድ ዕችላለሁ?	Enie meheid echilalehu?	Can I go?
መሄድ፡ ትችላለህ?	Anite meheid-tichilaleh?	Can you go?
መሄድ፡ ዕንችላለን?	Egna meheid enchilalen?	Can we go?

Adjectives ቅጽሎች

English With Amharic meaning	Comparative English With Amharic meaning	Supererlative English With Amharic meaning
Bad Metifo መጥፎ፡	Worse Betam metfo በጣም መጥፎ	Worst Ejig betam metfo ዕጅግ በጣም መጥፎ
Good Tiru ጥሩ	Better Betam tiru በጣም ጥሩ	Best Ejig betam tiru ዕጅግ በጣም ጥሩ
Old Arogie አሮጌ	Older Betam Arogie በጣም አሮጌ	Oldest Ejig betam arogie ዕጅግ በጣም አሮጌ
Little Tinish ትንሽ	Less Betam tinish በጣም ትንሽ	Least Ejig betam tinish ዕጅግ በጣም ትንሽ
Much Yebelete	More በጣም የበለጠ	Most ዕጅግ
Cheap	Betam yebelete	በጣም የበለጠ

የበለጠ ርካሽ	Cheaper	Ejig betam yebelete
በጣም ርካሽ		Cheapest
		ዕጅግ
		በጣም ርካሽ
Cheap	Cheaper	Cheapest
Rikash	Betam Rikash	Ejig betam rikash
ርካሽ	በጣም ርካሽ	ዕጅግ
		በጣም ርካሽ

Verb / ግስ

"Let us means - " ዕን..."

Verbs are words that express an action or occurrence. When you want to perform an action you say:" Let us....." In Amharic "Let us means " ዕን"..." So when you say:" Let us '', you are going to perform an action with another person. The same thing is true in Amharic. When you say:" " ዕን..." you are initiating some one to do some thing with you. Look at the following examples.

English	Amharic reading	Amharic meaning
Let us go	Enihid	ዕንሂድ
Let us eat	Enbila	ዕንብላ
Let us drink	Eniteta	ዕንጠጣ
Let us move	enkesakes	ዕንቀሳቀስ
Let us dance	enidenis	ዕንደንስ
Let us visit	enigobign	ዕንጎብኝ
Let us pay	enikifel	ዕንክፈል
Let us rest	Eniref	ዕንረፍ
Let us talk	eninegager	ዕንነጋገር

203

Questions/ጥያቄዎች

English	Reading	Amharic Meaning
Who?	mann?	ማን ?
Who is?	Mann neuw?	ማን ነው?
Who is a thief?	mann neuw leba?	ማን ነው ሌባ?
Which?	yetignaw?	የትኛው?
Which one is good?	yetignaw neuw tiru?	ጥሩ የትኛው ነው?
Where?	Yet/ wodet?	የት/ወዴት?
Where is?	Yet neuw?	የት ነው?
Where is?	Wedet neuw?	ወዴት ነው?
Where is the airport?	Yet neuw ayer mengedu?	የት ነው አየር መንገዱ?
	Wedet neuw ayer mengedu?	ወዴት ነው አየር መንገዱ?
Where is the airport?	Wedet neuw ayer mengedu?	አየር መንገዱ ወዴት ነው?
When?	mechie	መቼ?
When does the plane leave?	Mechie neuw planeu yemihedew?	መቼ ነው አውሮፕላኑ የሚሄደው?
How do you come?	Enidet?	እንዴት
	Endiet metah?	እንዴት መጣህ
Why?	Lemin?	ለምን
Why is it?	Silemin?	ስለምን ነው?

Why do I pay much?	Silemin bizu ikefilalehu?	ዕኔ ስለምን ብዙ ዕከፍላለሁ?
How much?	Sinit?	ስንት?
How much water?	Min yahil wuha?	ምን፡ያህል፡ ውሀ?
Too much water	Bizu wuha	ብዙ፡ ውሀ
How many?	Sinit?	ስንት?
How many buses?	Sinit autobisoch?	ስንት አውቶቢሶች?

To build your Amharic Language here with, more samples are given.

Sentences ዐረፍተ ነገሮች

Give me one birr	Lenie anid birr sitegn ለኔ አንድ ብር ስጠኝ
Across the street	Bemenigedu bashager በመንገዱ ባሻገር
Cheap	Rikash ርከሽ
The hotel across the street is cheap.	Bemenigedu bashager yalew hotel rikash neuw በመንገዱ፡ባሻገር፡ያለው፡ሆትየል፡ ርከሽ፡ ነው፡፡
Three people are sick.	Sosit sewoch tamewal ሶስት፡ሰወች፡ ተአመዋል፡፡
Four breasts	Arat tutoch አራት ጡቶች
A cow has four breasts.	Anid lam arat tutoch Aluwat አንድ፡ላም፡አራት ጡቶች፡ አሉዋት፡

English	Transliteration / Amharic
Man has got five fingers.	Sew amisit tatoch alut ሰው፡አምስት፡ ጣቶች፡ አሉት፡፡
Six is even number.	Sdist mulu kutir neuw ስድስት፡ሙሉ፡ ቁጥር፡ ነው፡፡
Holy spirit	Menifes kidus መንፈስ ቅዱስ
Seven is number of Holy Spirit.	Sebat yemenifes kidus kutir neuw ሰባት የመንፈስ ቅዱስ ቁጥር ነው
The figure has got eight sides.	Kirisu siminit gonoch alut ቅርጹ፡ ስምንት ፡ጎኖች ፡አሉት፡፡
Three times three is nine. 3x3=9	Sosit sibaza besosit zetegn 3x3= 9 ሶስት፡ሲባዛ፡በሶስትይሆናል ዘጠኝ፡፡
Rock – hewn church	Ke'anid dingia yetesera bete kiristian ከአንድ፡ድንጋይ፡ የተሠራ፡ ቤተ፡ክርስቲያን
After ten days	Ke'asir ken behuala ከአስር ቀን በሁዋላ
I will visit	Egobegnalehu ዕጎበኛለሁ
I will visit the rock-hewn Church of Lalibela	ke'anid dingia yeteserawin lalibela betekiristian egobegnalehu ከአንድ፡ድንጋይ፡የተሰራ ፡ቤተክርስቲያን ዕጎበኛለሁ
Wander	Asidenaki አስደናቂ
Lalibela	Lalibela ላሲበላ

Eighth wander	Siminitegna Asidenaki	ስምንተኛ አስደናቂ
of the world	ke'alem	ከአለም
Church	Betekiristian	ቤተክርስቲያን
You are our guest.	enanite engidoch nachihu	እናንተ፡ እንግዶቻችን፡ናችሁ
You are a traveler.	anite menigedegna neh	አንተ፡መንገደኛ፡ ነህ፡፡
You are a smart person.	Anite bilih sew neh	አንተ፡ብልህ፡ ሰው ፡ነህ፡፡
It is a dog.	Esu wusha neuw	እሱ፡ ውሻ ፡ነው
It is a cat.	Esu dimet neuw	እሱ፡ድመት፡ ነው፡፡
It is a cow.	Esua lam nat	እስዋ፡ ላም፡ ናት፡፡
He is a teacher.	Esu asitemari neuw	እሱ፡አስተማሪ፡ ነው፡፡
She is a singer.	Esua zefagn nat	እስዋ፡ዘፋኝ ፡ናት፡፡
They are farmers.	Enesu geberewoch nachew	እነሱ፡ ገበሬዎች፡ ናቸው፡፡
This is a book.	yih mestahaf neuw	ይህ መጽሐፍ ነው
That is a sheep.	ya beg neuw	ያ፡ በግ፡ ነው፡፡
These are goats.	enezih fiyeloch nachew	እነዚህ፡ፍየሎች፡ ናቸው፡፡
Those are tables.	enezia terepezawoch nachew	እነዚያ፡ጠረጴዛዎች፡ ናቸው፡፡

Time

English	Amharic
After	Behuala / በሁዋላ
Before	befit / በፊት
Now	Ahun / አሁን
Tomorrow	Nege / ነገ
Yesterday	Tinant / ትናንት
An hour ago	Ke-anid se'at befit / ከአንድ ሰአት በፊት
Mid day	ekule ken / (ዕኩለ፡ቀን)
Afternoon	Ke se'at behuala / ከሰአት በሁዋላ
In the morning	Betuat / በጡዋት
In the evening	Bemishit / በምሽት
Tonight	Zare mishit / ዛሬ ምሽት
Yesterday evening	Tenantmishit / ትናንት ምሽት
Early morning	Betuat/ bemaleda / በጡዋት፡ (በማለዳ)
Before dinner	Kerat befit / ከራት በፊት
After lunch	Kemisa behuala / ከምሳ በሁዋላ
Now let us go	Ahun enihid / አሁን ዕንሂድ
Until mid day	Esike ekule ken / ዕስከ ዕኩለ ቀን

Shopping words

Sint neuw? ስንት ነው?	How much is it?
Meshet መሸጥ	To sell
Hulet acketoch amita ሁለት ፓኬቶች አምጣ	Bring two packets
Mels መልስ	Change
Gebeya ገበያ	Market
Ruz ሩዝ	rice
Waga ዋጋ	price
Birr ብር	birr
Hisab ሂሳብ	bill/ account
Tekilala ጠቅላላ	total
Packet ፓኬት	Packet
Yemigib medebir የምግብ መደብር	Food shop
Melisun wused መልሱን ውሰድ	Keep the change
Ameseginalehu አመሰግናለሁ	Thank you.
Suk ሱቅ	Shop
Liyu-liyu ልዩልዩ	Different
አይነት ayinet	Kinds
ልዩልዩ አይነት liyu liyu ayinet	Miscellaneous
Rikash ርከሽ	Cheap
Widd/ውድ	Expensive
Kibidet ሚዛን	Weight

Hulunim mezin ሁሉንም መዝን	Weight every thing
Shai ሻይ	Tea
Bunna ቡና	Coffee
Dabo ዳቦ	Bread
Wuha ዉሀ	Water
Sikuwar ስኩዋር	Sugar
Mar ማር	Honey
Injera ዕንጀራ	Injera
Soda ሶዳ	Soda
Duket ዱቄት	Flour
Abeba አበባ	Flower
Samuna ሳሙና	Soap
Medihanit መድሀኒት	Medicine
Woreket ወረቀት	Paper
Yeshinit bet woreket የሽንት ቤት ወረቀት	Toilet paper
Tekilala waga ጠቅላላ ዋጋ	total price
ድምር Dimir	Sum
ሁለት መቶ ሀያ ብር Hulet meto haya birr	two hundred twenty birr
አንድ ነገር ረሳሁ Anid neger resahu	I forget one more thing.
ምንድን ነው? Mindin neuw?	What is that?
ወጥ መስሪያ ብረት ድስት Wott-mesiria biret disit	Cooking pan for wott
Minayinet? ምን አይነት	What kind?

ሁለት ሊትር የሚይዝ ትልቅ ድስት Hulet liter yemiyiz tilik disit	Big cooking pan that contains two liters
Zarie yelenim ዛሬ የለንም	Today we do not have it.

Punctuation
Netboch (ነጥቦች)

Period in English [.)In Amharic is like like [::] or four dots. Four dots in Amharic-means-aratnetiboch; is written:[አራት፡ ነጥቦች] in Amharic.In both languages You put them at the end of a sentence.

Leave space between each word
In English leave a small space between each word. Example: John rides a horse. (.) You put a period at the end of a sentence.

፡ ፡ አራት ነጥቦች፡
በአረፍተ፡ነገር፡
መጨረሻ ነው፡፡
ምሳሌ፡ አበበ ፈረስ ጋለበ፡፡

Two dots
፡ ሁለት፡ነጥቦች፡
ሁለት፡ ነጥቦች፡
በየእንዳንዱ
ቃል፡መጨረሻ፡ላይ፡
ጻፍ ፡፡
/፡ ፡/ አራት ነጥቦች
በአረፍተ ነገር
መጨረሻ

211

Question Mark-(?) Question mark: is at the end of a direct question both in English and Amharic. Example: What is your name?	የጥያቄ የጥያቄ ምልክት (?) በዕንግሊዝኛም፡ሆነ፡ በአማርኛ፡ የጥያቄ፡ ምልክት፡፡በመጨረሻ፡ ይገኛል፡፡ ምሳሌ፡ አንተ፡ ምሳ ፡በላህ ወይ?
Exclamation point (!) You put an exclamation point after words or phrases or sentences to express shock. Example – Help! Help!	የቃለ አጋኖ ምልክት፡ ምሳሌ ዕርዳተአ! በአማርኛ ፡ሰው ዕሪ፡ ከለ፡ በጣም፡ችግር፡ላይ፡ ነው ማለት፡ነው፡፡ ሰው፡ሌገድላው፡ ይሆናል ተብሎ፡ ይገመትአል፡፡
Quotation Mark - is same as in English. There is no much difference. Example: He said: "I like bread".	የጥቅስ፡ምልክት " " Yetikis Milikit ልክ ዕንደ ዕንግሊዝኛው ነው፡፡ ተመሳሳይ ነው፡፡ ብዙ ልዩነት የለውም፡፡ ምሳሌ "ዕሱ፡ዳቦ ዕወዳለሁ አለ፡፡"
Quotation is written in between / " "/	የጥቅስ፡ምልክት / Yetikis Milikit በአማርኛ የሚጻፈው፡በነዚህ ምልክቶች " " መከከል ነው፡፡

Forms of be

The two major forms of **BE**: *is* and *are*. Forms of **be** work in coordination with pronouns like: I, we, you, he, she, it and they. Forms of **be** have tenses, namely; presnt tense, past tense and future tense

Forms of **be**- Present tense

Present Tense	Short form	Negative form
ያሁን ጊዜ	በአጭር ፎርም	በአሉታ ፎርም
		ዕኔ አይደለሁም
I am	I 'm	I 'm not
ዕኔ ነኝ	ዕኔ ነኝ	ዕኔ ːአይደለሁም
You are	You're	You aren't
አንተ ነህ	አንተ ነህ	አንተ አይደለህ
He is	He's	He isn't
ዕሱ ነው	ዕሱ ነው	ዕሱ አይደለም
She is	She's	she isn't
ዕስዋ ናት	ዕስዋ ናት	ዕስዋ አይደለችም
It is	It's	It isn't
ዕሱ ነው /ለዕቃ/	ዕሱ ነው /ለዕቃ/	ዕሱ አይደለም
We are	We're	We aren't
ዕኛ ነን	ዕኛ ነን	ዕኛ አይደለንም
You are	You 're	You aren't
አንተ ነህ	አንተ ነህ	ዕናንተ አይደላችሁም
They are	They 're	They aren't
ዕነሱ ናቸው	ዕነሱ ናቸው	ዕነሱ አይደሉም

Forms of BE --Past tense

Past Tense ሀላፊ፡ጊዜ	Short form በአጭር ፎርም	Negative form በአሉተአ ፎርም
I was ዕኔ ነበርሁ	I was ዕኔ ነበርሁ	I wasn't ዕኔ ፡አልነበርሁም
You were አንተ ነበርህ	You were አንተ ነበርህ	You weren't አንተ አልነበርህም
He was ዕሱ ነበር	He was ዕሱ ነው	He wasn't ዕሱ አልነበረም
She was ዕስዋ ነበረች	She was ዕስዋ ነበረች	She wasn't ዕስዋ አልነበረችም
It was ዕሱ፡ነው ለዕቃ	It was ዕሱ ነበር ለዕቃ	It wasn't ዕሱ አልነበረም
We were ዕኛ ነን	We were ዕኛ ነበርን	We weren't ዕኛ አልነበርንም
You were አንተ ነህ	You were አንተ ነበርህ	You weren't ዕናንተ አልነበራችሁም
They were ዕንሱ ነበሩ	They were ዕነሱ አልነበሩም	They aren't ዕነሱ አልነበሩም

Grammar Construction

I	Pronoun
ዕኔ	ተውላጠ ስም

Verb	Noun	Adverb
ግስ	ስም	ተውሳከ ግስ
eat	Dinner	well
መብላት	ምሳ	ደህና
		well
		ደህና

In Amharic you write a sentence like this.

Pronoun	Noun	adverb	Verb
Enie	Missa	Dehina	Belahu
ዕኔ	ምሳ	ደህና	በላሁ
Egna	Missa	dehina	Belan
ዕኛ	ምሳ	ደህና	በላን
Ante	Missa	dehina	Belah
አንተ	ምሳ	ደህና	በላህ
Anchi	Missa	dehina	Belash
አንቺ	ምሳ	ደህና	በላሽ
Enante	Missa	dehina	Belachihu
ዕናንተ	ምሳ	ደህና	በላችሁ
Esu	Missa	dehina	bela
ዕሱ	ምሳ	ደህና	በላ
Esua	Missa	dehina	Belach
ዕስዋ	ምሳ	ደህና	በላች
Enesu	Missa	dehina	Belu
ዕነሱ	ምሳ	ደህና	በሉ
Esu	Missa	dehina	bela
ዕሱ	ምሳ	ደህና	በላ

* In English female is a lady.
* In Amharic it is seit. /ሴት/ is a female or a lady.
* In English male is a man.
* In Amharic wond /ወንድ/ is a male or a man

English	Amharic
Present tense Ye- ahun gize	Ye- ahun gize የአሁን ጊዜ
Am ነኝ	Enie Negn ዕኔ ነኝ
Are ናችሁ	Enanite Nachihu ዕናንተ ናችሁ
Is ነው	Esu Nuew ዕሱ ነው

English	Amharic	Amharic
Positive	Awonta	አወንተአ
There was	Neber	ነበር
There was a man.	Anid sew neber	አንድ ሰው ነበር
There were	Neberu	ነበሩ
There were a few camels.	Tikit Gimeloch neberu	ጥቂት ግመሎች ነበሩ
Question	Tiyake	ጥያቄ
Was there	Neber?	ነበር?
Were there some sites?	Neberu? Yemitayu botawoch neberu?	የሚተአዩ ቦተአወች ነበሩ?

English	English	Amharic	Amharic
I	Am	Enie ዕኔ	Negn ነኝ
We	Are	Egna ዕኛ	Nen ነን
You Male	are	Ante አንተ	Neh ነህ
You Female	are	Anchi አንቺ	Nesh ነሽ
You	are	Enante ዕናንተ	Nachihu ናችሁ
He	is	Esu ዕሱ	Neuw ነው
She	is	Esua ዕሱዋ	Nat ናት
They	are	Enesu ዕነሱ	Nachew ናቸው
It Male	is	Esu ዕሱ	Neuw ነው
It Female	IS	Esua ዕሱዋ	Nat ናት

Am not/ Are not/is not

	English	Amharic
I	am not	Enie-ayidelehum ዕኔ አይደለሁም
He	is not	esu ayidelem ዕሱ አይደለም
She	is not	esua ayidelechim ዕስዋ አይደለችም
It	is not	esu ayidelem ዕሱ አይደለም
James	is not	James-ayidelem ጄምስ አይደለም
You/ female	are not	anchi

		ayideleshim አንቺ:አይደለችም
We	are not	Egna;ayidelenim ዕኛ አይደለንም
You	are not	Ante-ayidelehim አንተ አይደለህም
They	are not	Enesu-ayidelum ዕነሱ አይደሉም

There is/ there are.

Positive	Awonta
Awonta	አወንተአ
There is something	Anid neger alle
Anid neger alle	አንድ:ነገር አለ
There is a hotel	Anid hotel alle አንድ: ሆትየል: አለ
There are	Allu
Allu	አሉ
There are Many hotels.	Bizu hotelo-ch allu. ብዙ :ሆትየሎች: አሉ
Negative	Alluta/አሉተአ
There is not	Yelem/የለም
There is not a room	Anid kifil yelem አንድ ክፍል የለም
Eg.- A boy A=An=1	አንድ:ልጅ:: 1=አንድ= anid
There is not	Yelum የለም
There are not many people	Bizu sew-och yellum ብዙ ሰወች የሉም

218

Question forms of "is there/are there?"

English	Amharic
Is there? For something	Allen? Meaning አለን? ለአንድ ነገር
Is there some water?	Tinish-wuha allen? ትንሽ ውሀ አለን?
Are there?	Allun? አሉን?
Are there some books?	Tikit mestahifit allun? ጥቂት መጻህፍት ፡አሉን?

Positive sentences
ቀጥተኛ አረፍተ ነገር

English	Amharic
Go straight [for male]	Ketita hid. ቀጥተአ ሂድ
Go straight [for female]	Ketita hiji ቀጥተአ ሂጂ
Come on [for male]	Na ና
Come on [female]	Ney ነይ
Turn left [for male]	Wode gira zur ወደ ግራ ዙር
Turn left [for female]	Wode gira zuri ወደ ግራ ዙሪ
Turn right [for male]	Wode kegn zur ወደ ቀኝ ዙር

219

Turn right [for female]	Wode kegn zuri ወደ ቀኝ ዙሪ
Stand up [for male]	Kum ቁም
Stand up [for female]	Kumi ቁሚ
Sit down [for male]	Tekemet ተቀመጦ
Sit down [for female]	Tekemechi ተቀመጪ
Drink some coffee- male	Tinsh bunateta ትንሽ ቡና ጠጣ
Drink some coffee[for [female]	Tinish buna techi ትንሽ ፡ቡና ጠጪ
Listen for [male]	Sima ስማ
Listen for [female]	Simi ስሚ
Buy some gazeta for [male]	Gazeta giza ጋዜጣ ግዛ
Buy some gazeta for [female]	Gazeta giji ጋዜጣ ግጊር
Gazeta = news paper. No gender	Gazeta = gazeta ጋዜጣ

Numbers ቁጥሮች

Arabic Numbers	Translation in English	Translation in Amharic
1	one	anid አንድ
2	two	Hulet ሁለት
3	three	sosit ሶስት
4	four	Arat አራት
5	five	Amisit አምስት
6	six	Sidist ስድስት
7	seven	Sebat ሰባት
8	eight	Siminit ስምንት
9	nine	Zetegn ዘጠኝ
10	ten	Asir አስር
11	*Eleven*	Asira anid አስራ አንድ
12	*twelve*	Asirahulet አስራ ሁለት
Teen	*13-19*	Asira አስራ (ke 11-19) (ከ11-19)
13	*Thirteen*	Misale 13 ምሳሌ ፡ (13) =አስራ ሶስት
20	twenty	Haya ሀያ
30	thirty	Selasa ሠላሳ
40	forty	Ariba አርባ
50	fifty	Amisa አምሳ
60	sixty	Silisa ስልሳ
70	seventy	Seba ሰባ
80	eighty	Semaniya ሰማኒያ

90	Ninety	Zetena ዘጠና
100	One hundred	Anid meto አንድ መቶ
101	One hundred one	Anid meto anid አንድ መቶ አንድ
200	Two hundred	Hulet meto ሁለት መቶ
300	Three hundred	Sosit meto ሶስት መቶ
400	Four hundred	Arat Meto አራት መቶ
500	Five hundred	Amist Meto አምስት መቶ
600	Six hundred	Sidist Meto ስድስት መቶ
700	Seven hundred	Sebat Meto ሰባት መቶ
800	Eight hundred	Semint Meto ስምንት መቶ
900	Nine hundred	Zetegn Meto ዘጠኝ መቶ
1000	One thousand	Anid Shi አንድ ሺ
2000	Two Thousand	Hulet Shi ሁለት ሺ

The pre-fix /bale ባለ shows possession

English	Transliteration / Amharic
We are owners of the hotel.	egna yehoteyelu balebetoch nen እኛ የሆትየሉ፡ ባለቤቶች፡ ነን፡፡
Owner of the bed	Bale'aliga ባለ አልጋ
Founding father	Balabat ባላባት
well known person	Balabat ባላባት
A person who gets salary	bale'demewoz ባለ ደመወዝ
A person who has land	Bale meret ባለመሬት
A person who has income	Bale gebi ባለገቢ
A person who has a house	Balebet ባለቤት
A person who has a shop	Balesuq ባለሱቅ
A person who has a travelling bag	Bale-shanta በለሻንጣ
Aperson who has money	Bale-gnizeb ባለገንዘብ

Chapter 8
To practice reading in Amharic
Queen Sheba ንግሥተ፡ሳባ

ንግሥተ፡ሳባ፡የኢትዮጵያ ንግሥት፡ዕግዚአብሔርን፡ በመጀመሪያ፡አታውቅም፡ ነበር፡፡	Sheba was a Gentile queen of Ethiopia.
በህይወትዋ፡የዕግዚአብሔርን፡ ድንቅና፡ተአምር፡አይትአ፡ አታውቅም፡ ነበር፡፡	She didn't see a single miracle in her life.
ዕስዋ፡ግን፡የዕግዚአብሔርን፡ ጥበብ፡ለማየት፡ትጉዋጉዋ፡ ነበር፡፡	She was eager to see the Wisdom of God.
ዕስዋ፡ግን፡የዕግዚአብሔርን፡ ቃል፡መስማት፡ትፈልግ፡ ነበር፡፡	She was eager to hear the Word of God.
ዕስዋም፡የሰሎሞንን፡ጥበብ፡ ለመስማት፡ወደ፡ሩቅ፡አገር፡ ተጉዋዘች፡፡	She traveled a long distance to hear the Wisdom of Solomon.
ዕስዋ፡ጌታ፡በመሬት፡ላይ፡ በነበረበት፡ጊዜ፡አለኖረችም፡፡	She did not live in the days of the Lord.
ዕስዋም፡የዕግዚብኔርን፡ ሃያል ሥራ፡ አላየችም፡፡	She didn't see supernatural works of God.
ዕስዋም፡ክርስቶስ፡ በተወለደበት፡ በመጀመሪያው፡መቶ፡ክፍለ፡	No doubt she would have readily received Jesus had she

ዘመን፡ኑራ፡ ቢሆን፡ ክርስቶስን፡ ዕንደምትቀበል፡አንድም፡ የሚያጠራጥር፡ነገር፡የለም፡፡ ዕስዋም፡ለክርስቶስ፡ስላላት፡ ፍቅር፡

የዕግዚአብሔር፡ፈቃድም፡ ዕስዋን፡በፍርድ፡ቀን፡ በሀጢአተኞች፡ላይ፡ዕሱን፡ በተውት፡ላይ፡ ዕንድትፈርድ፡ያስነሳትአል፡፡ ከሰሎሞን፡የሚበልጥ፡ከዚህ፡ አለ፡፡

lived in the 1st century A.D.

It was because of her zeal of her zeal for Christ, It is God's will to rise her up in judgement against those wicked who rejected Him and behold! There is Someone thing greater than Solomon is here. (Luke 11:31)

666 is the Devil itself.
666፡ራሱ፡ሰይጣን፡ነው፡፡

የአማርኛ፡ ትርጉም	English translation
ስድስት፡ስድስት፡ይህ፡ሰይጣን፡መሆኑ፡ነው፡፡ትላለህ፡፡ በዚያን፡ ጊዜ፡ የጌትአን፡ ስም፤ ጥራ፡፡ ሰይጣኑ፡ ይሸሻል፡፡ የጌትአን፡ስም፡የሚጠራ፡ ይድናል፡ ተብሎ፡ ተጽፎአል፡፡	When you see 6 & 6 & 6 You might think of an evil thing. So call the name of Jesus. The evil will go away. It is written that those who call the name of Jesus will be saved.
666 ራሱ፡ ሰይጣኑ፡ነው፡፡ በየሱስ፡ ስም! ከዚህ፡ ጥፋ!	666 is the Devil himself. In Jesus name, go away!

666 is a scary one.
666፡የሚዘገንን፡ ነገር፡ነው፡፡

ማንም፡ጨለማ፡ አይወድም፡፡	Nobody-likes darkness.
ጨለማ፡የሰይጣን፡ ምልክት፡ ነው፡፡	Darkness is a symbol of evil spirit.
ዕግዚአብሄር፡ራሱ፡ ጨለማ፡ አይውድም፡፡ ጨለማ፡ዕንዲወገድ፡ ብርሃን፡ ዕንዲመጣ፡ አዞአልና፡፡	God Himself does not like darkness. He commanded light to shine out of darkness.

Satan is a killer

ሰይጣን፡ ነፍስ- ገዳይ፡ነው፡፡

ሰይጣን፡ነፍስ ገዳይ፡ ነው፡፡	Satan is a killer.
ስለዚህ፡ከመሞትህ፡ በፊት፡ኢየሱን፡ ፈልገው፡፡	So before you die seek Jesus.
መጽሐፍ፡ቅዱስን፡ አንብብ፡፡	Read the Bible
ተዘጋጅ፡፡የደስትአ፡ ኑሮ ለመኖር፡መመሪያ፡ አግኝ፡፡	Get ready. Get instruction. to enjoy life
መጽሐፍ፡ ቅዱስ፡ሊረዳህ፡ዝግጁ፡ ነው፡፡	Bible is ready to help.
ለምን?መጽሐፍ፡ ቅዱስ? ምክንያቱም፡መጽሐፍ፡ ቅዱስ፡መጽሐፍ፡ ቅዱስ፡ነው፡፡	Why Bible? Because it is B-I-B-L-E-
ምን፡ማለትህ፡ነው? ማለት፡መመሪያ፡ይሰጣል፡፡ ሰይጣን፡ ሳይገድልሕ፡ መጀመሪያ፡ዕንዴት፡ መፅንፍ፡ቅዱስ፡ ይሰጣል፡፡ መፅንፍ፡ቀዱስ፡ምንድን፡ ነው? ማወቅ፡ትፈልጋለሕ? ተመልከት፡፡	B-I-B-L-E- gives instruction before Satan takes you to hell. How does it give? What is Bible? O! Do you want to know what it means? Bible is a five letter word. B-I-B-L-E. means:-
መጽሐፍ፡ ቀዱስ፡፡ የምንመራበት በፊት	B- Means Book of I- means instruction B- mean before

ከመልቀቃችን	L--means leaving
መሬትን መጽሃፍ ቅዱስ: መሬትን :ከመልቀቃችን በፊት: የምንመራበት መጽሃፍ:ነው::	E--means Earth. Together Bible means- "Book of instruction before leaving the earth."

Jesus makes intercession
ኢየሱስ:ያማልዳል
(ሮሜ:8:34) (Romans 8: 34)

የብዙ:ሰወችን ሀጢአት:ተሸከመ:: (ኢሳያስ:53:12) ስለአመጻኞችም: ማለደ:: (ኢሳያስ:53:12)	Jesus suffered for our sins See-Isaih 53:12 He asked God to forgive us. See- Isaih 53:12
ኢየሱስ:በሰውና: በእግዚአብሔር: መከከል:አማላጅ: ነው:: ሮሜ :8:34::	Jesus is the mediator between man and God. Romans 8: 34.
ኢየሱስ: በእግዚአብሔር:አብ: ቀኝ: ተቀምጦ: ስለእኛ :ያማልዳል:: ሮሜ:8:34 ዕና: ዕብራውያን:7:25: ተመልከት::	Being at God's right side He speaks on our behalf. (Rome -8:34 and Heb. 7:25)

More explanations about life
ስለሕይወት፡ የሚያስፈልጉ፡ብዙ፡ገለጻወች

የአማርኛ፡ትርጉም	English translation
ሕይወት፡ደስት እ፡ ነዉ።፡፡ ተገናኘዉ ።	Life is a challenge. Meet it
ልጅ፡መዉለድ፡ ድስተእ፡ ነዉ።፡፡	To give birth to a baby is happiness. Enjoy it.
ሕይወት፡ስጦት እ፡ ነዉ።፡፡ ተቀበለዉ።፡፡	Life is a gift. Accept it
ሕይወት፡መከራ፡ ነዉ።፡፡ተጋፈጠዉ።፡፡	Life is tragedy. Face it.
ሕይወት፡ሥራ፡ ነዉ።፡፡አከናዉነዉ።፡፡	Life Is duty. Perform it.
ሕይወት፡ጨዋት እ ነዉ።፡፡ተጫወተዉ።፡፡	Life is a game. Play it.
ሕይወት፡ መዝሙር፡ነዉ።፡ ዘምረዉ።፡፡	Life is a song. Sing it to glorify the Lord. When I am weak, I am strong. Grace is my shield, Christ my song
ሕይወት ዕድል ነዉ።፡፡ ዉሰደዉ።፡፡	Life is an opportunity. Take it.
ሕይወት ጉዞ ነዉ።፡፡ ጨርሰዉ።፡፡	Life is a journey Complete it.
ሕይወት ቃል ኪዳን ነዉ።፡፡ፈጽመዉ።፡፡	Life is promise. Fulfill it.
ሕይወት፡ዉበት ነዉ።፡፡ አመስግነዉ።፡፡	Life is a beauty. Praise it.

ህይወት:ትግል: ነዉ:: ተአገለዉ::	Life is a struggle. Wrestle it.
ህይወት:ግብ ነዉ::አግኘዉ::	Life is a goal. Achieve it.
ህይወት ዕንቆቅልሽ :ነዉ:: ፍትአዉ::	Life is a puzzle. Solve it.
ህይወት :ፍቅር ነዉ:: ዉደደዉ:: መኪና:ያስ ዘይት: ይሞቃል::ከዚያም: አደጋ: ያጋጥምሃል:: ዕንደዚሁም: ሰዉችን: ከልወደድህ: ራስህ: በጭንቀት: ተሰቃይተህ: ብቸኛ: ሆነህ: ራስን:ጠልተህ: ትሰቃያለህ::	Life is love. Love it. With out oil the axle of your car will be hot and soon you will have accident. In the same token if you do not love people, you will hate yourself and then you will suffer loneliness and depression
የሱስ:አለ:: ዕኔ መንገድና:ዕዉነት: ህይወትም:ነኝ: (ዮሐንስ:14:6--ይህም ማለት:-- ዕየሱስ:መንገድ ነዉ:: አየሱስ:ዕዉነት: ነዉ):: 1) በኢየሱስ ክርስቶስ: ብትአምን	"Jesus is the way, the truth and the life." John 14:6. This means:-* Jesus Himself is the way. * Jesus Himself is the Truth * Jesus Himself is Life. 1) If you believe in Jesus, He will give you the strength of a young eagle. Psalm 103:5 2) If you believe in Jesus Christ you won't be punished.

ኅልማስነትህን
፡ዕንደንስር፡ ያድሳል፡፡
መዝሙር፡- 103:5

2)በክርስቶስ፡
ኢየሱስ፡ያለዉ
፡የህይወት፡መንፈስ፡ህግ
፡ከሃጢአትና፡
ክሞት፡ ህግአርነት፡
አዉቶናልና፡፡
ሮሜ. 8:1-2
ኢየሱስ ህይወት
ነዉ፡፡
1ኛ ዮሐንስ 1:5

Holy Spirit will give you life that comes from Christ Jesus and will set you free from sin and death. Rom. 8:1-2
God is light
Jesus is life.
1st John 1:5

English Amharic Translations

የአማርኛ ትርጉም	English/translation
ሰማያዊ/semayawi	heavenly
ጥቅም/ጠቃሚ	benefit
ከዚህ በትአች	herewith
መሬት/meret	earth
የሰማያዊ አከላት yesemayawi akalat	Heavenly bodies
ሰማይ/semay	Sky
ስላሴ/Silasie	Trinity
አብ/Ab	Father
ወልድ/Wold	Son
መንፈስ ቅዱስ Menfes Kidus	Holy Spirit
ከአዕምሮ በላይ ke-aemiro belay	Transcends one's mind
የዕግዚአብሄር፡ሃሳብ Ye-egzi-abher-hasab	The idea of God
መገለጥ/megelet	reveal
ትልቅነት/ tilikenet	Greatness
መፍጠር/ mefiter	Create
ብዙ/bizu	Multitude
ተፈጥሮ/tefetiro	Nature

አማርኛ ትርጉም	English translation
ማስደሰት (ግስ)	Please
ደስ፡ የሚያሰኝ (ስም)	Please (V)
	Pleasant (noun)
መውደቅ	Fail
መዋሸት	Lie
የማያምን	unbeliever
የትም ቦትአ	everywhere
ሁሉም ነገር	Everything
ጊዜ	Time
ባዶ ቦታአ	Space
ቁሳአከል	Matter
ሶስት ነገሮች	Triad
አ ሁን	Present (now)
ያለፈ ጊዜ	Past
የወደፊት	Future
ቁመት	Length
ወርድ	Breadth
ከፍተአ	Height
ጉልበት	Energy
ዕንቅስቃሴ	Motion
ክስተት	Phenomenon
ክስተቶች	Phenomena
ጸሀይ	Sun
ብርሀን	Light
ሙቀት	Heat
መንፈስ	Spirit
ነፍስ	Soul
አከል/ሰዉነት	Body

Things to know about God.

ስለዕግዚአብሔር፡ ማወቅ፡ የሚያስፈልጉት፡ ነገሮች፡

እሱ አይዋሽም	He never lies.
እሱ አይወድቅም	He never fails.
እሱ በማያምን ሰው፡አይደሰትም	He is never interested in an unbeliever

Triad things to know

God is

ዕግዚአብሔር ነው

ክቡር	Glorious
ጻድቅ	Righteous.
ቅዱስ	Holy.

Universe is a relationship

ሀዋ፡ አከል፡የሶስት፡ነገሮች፡ዝምድና፡ነው።፡

ጊዜ	Time
ባዶ ቦታ	Space
ቁስአከል	Matter

Matter is a relation of:-

ቁስአከል:-

የጠጠረ:ነገር	Solid
ፈሳሽ	Liquid
ጋዝ	Gas

Three dimensions of space

የቦትአ: ሶስት: አንግሎች:አሉት::

ቁመት	Length
ወርድ	Breadth
ከፍተአ	Height.

Three natures of the Sun

ጸሀይ ሶስት:ባህሪያት: አሉዋት::

*ሙቀት—እንዱ:የጸሀይ ተፈጥሮ ነው
*Heat:- is one of the three characters of the sun.
(Psalm 19:6)

ብርሀን	light
ሀይል	energy
ሙቀት	heat

234

Trinity.- Three nature of God.

ስላሴ:የዕግዚአብሔር: ሶስት:ባህሪያት

ዕግዚአብሔር፡ አብ	God the Father
ዕግዚአብሔር፡ ወልድ	God the Son
ዕግዚአብሔር፡ መንፈስ :ቅዱስ	God Holy Spirit

God creates man in His own image.

ዕግዘአብሔር:ሰውን: በአምሳሉ:ፈጠረ::
(See: Gen. 1:26)

ስጋ	Body/ Flesh
ነፍስ	Soul
መንፈስ	Spirit.
ሽክላ	pot
ሽክላ ሠሪ	potter
ሰው ሽክላ ነው::	man is the pot
ዕግዘአብሔር:	The Lord
ሽክላ ሠሪ	is the potter

For further knowledge – Read Potter's House by Wallace H. Helfin, Jr.

Matter consists of three things.
ቁሰአከል ፡ ሶስት፡ነገሮችን ፡ይዘአል፡፡

ሀይል	Energy
ዕንቅስቃሴ	Motion
ክስተት	Phenomenon

Time consists of three things.
ጊዜ፡ሶስት፡ነገሮችን ፡ይዘአል፡፡

ያሁን ጊዜ	Present
ያለፈ ጊዜ	Past
የወደፊት ጊዜ	Future

Source:- Seeing Christ in the Old Testament: - by Ervin N. Hershberger published in 1999.

Three Patriarchs of ancient time
ሶስቱ፡የጥንት፡ አባቶች

አብራሀም	Abraham
ይስሀቅ	Isaac
ያዕቆብ	Jacob

Triad bodies of a government
ሶስቱ፡ የመንግስት፡ አከላት

ሥራ አስፈጻሚ ክፍል	Executive
ሕግ አዉጪ ክፍል	Legislative
የዳኝነት ክፍል	Judiciary

ሶስት፡ ምስክሮች፡አስተማማኝ ናቸው፡፡In the judiciary body witnesses of two, three or more are eliable.

Spiritual Fighting

መንፈሳዊ፡ ውጊያ   means- Spiritual fighting
መንፈሳዊ፡ውጊያ፡ሰዎች፡ጋር፡አይደለም፡፡
Spiritual fighting isn't against humans.
ውጊያው፡ከሰይጣን፡ጋር፡ነው፡፡
The fight is against evil.
ውጊያው፡ከጨለማ፡ሀይል፡
፡ጋር፡ነው፡፡ኤፌሶን፡6:10-17
The fight is against the power of the darkness.
See: Ephesians 6:10-17.
ጦሬ የምዋጋበት
My arms to fight with
ጋሻየ የምመከበት
My sword that I rely on
የማሸንፍበት
My armor of victory
ኢየሱስ፡ጉልበትና፡ሃይሌ፡ነው፡፡
Jesus is my power and strength.

Name of Al-Mighty God

የሕያሉ፡ ዕግዚአብኤር፡ስሞች፨

Elohim ኤሉሂም	My Creator የኔ ፈጣሪ /ፈጣሪየ/
Jehovah ጀሆቫ	My Lord የኔ፡አምላክ አምላኬ
El – Shaddai ኤልሻዳይ	My Supplier የኔ ሁሉን /አድራጊ/
Adonai አዶናይ	My Master ጌትአየ
Jehovah Jireh ጀሆቫ:ጀሪ	My Provider የኔ ሁሉን ሰጭ
Jehovah Rophe ጀሆቫ-ሮፌ	My healer ፈዋሼ
Jehovah Nessi ጀሆቫ-ነሲ	My Banner መከትአየ
Jehovah Mikkadesh ጀሆቫ-መቀዲሽ	My Sanctifier ቅድስናየ
Person Jehovah Tsidkenu ጀሆቫ- ጽዲኩኒ	My Righteous ጽድቄ

Jehovah Shalom Rohi ጆሆባ-ሻሎም	My Peace ሰላሜ
Jehovah Rohi ጆሆባ- ሮሂ	My Shepherd ዕረኛየ
Jehovah Shammah (ጆሆባ- ሻማ) means The Lord is there. See Ezek. 48:35)	አብሮ፡ኑዋሪየ /የማይለየኝ/ My Abiding Presence-This shows that the Lord is present all the time.

Sources: 1) A Brochure ''Seeing Christ'' sent to my home on Nov. 1/ 2007 by Pastor Benny Hinn.

Therefore; a person whose belief in the Lord is spotless could sings saying:

Jehovah,   You're my Savour.
 You're my Rebuilder.
 You're my Defender.
 You're my Healer.
 You're my Shepher.
 You're my Provider - Jahovah-Jireh

Check from Jesus

Check - *For those who follow Jesus.*

```
No .....Rom 3:10 , 29          Date Now... 2ⁿᵈ Corn.6:2
Bank of Eternal Life.......-resources unlimited

Pay to the order of ....Whosoever believes (John3:16) $Rom.6:23

Sum of Eternal life ___ Believe on the Lord Jesus Christ
and though shall be saved  ( Acts 16:31)
By Jesus Christ
Signature--- John 10:28
```

To order more tracts Use this address
Tracts
233 Jule Merck Rd
Norris, S.C. 29667

Salvation
Sinner's Prayer

If anyone thinks he is lost and believes that he is a sinner, there is a Word for him. Any one should not think that he is a vile. Nobody on earth was / is pure. Everybody who now thinks himself is a saint was once a sinner.

Nonetheless if you repent, you have hope. God hates sin. He loves sinners. Now if you say:" God forgive me", He will forgive you. So if you seek God, please pray this prayer:" Lord! I am a sinner. You died for the sinners and I am a sinner. After this God has forgiven your sin, and believe that.

After sincere prayer you're forgiven. You have joined the Kingdom of God. You're saved from the wrath of God. You're under the feet and protection of Jesus. Jesus is the builder of your fate. You're the temple of God. You're a good man in the eye of God.

Once you are saved from the wrath of God, you are expected by God Al-Mghty to pray for others, your family, neighbors, for people in your Church, for your country and for leaders in power. This book is about the visitation of Ethiopia by the Lord. If you pray, curse from our country will also be removed. Always it is also good to obey God of the Bible and the Lord of the Bible says:"Pray for kings and for those in power. (See 1st Timothy 2:1-2.)

God bless you

Conclusion

God made the earth and on the bank of the rivers agriculture started. In Ethiopia on both banks of the Blue Nile and probably along the banks of Awash River people started to settle down, to domesticate animals and to cultivate plants. In Ethiopia; though there are many rivers Blue Nile has always been through out the ages the major source of water supply for Egypt and the Sudan.

God – the rewarder- Hebrews 11:6

According to the Book of Hebrews, Chapter 11 a person who has faith in God does not die. Even though he dies in flesh he is alive in Spirit. According to the Book of Romans Chapter 8:1 if one belongs to Christ he is not punished. Take for example Enoch who had faith in God and who did not die. According to Hebrews 11:5 because Henock's faith pleased the Lord, God took him up to Heavens. Going to heaven is one thing. Getting rich in the world we live in is another thing.

In the world we live in, especially in the modern times the idea of opening business and getting money is spreading like wild fire. Christians on their behalf are highly interested in opening business. For those brothers and sisters who love and honour the Lord it is possible only when they obey God because the Lord says:"I am the Lord, All Powerful. So do not depend on your own power or strength, but on my Spirit." See Zechariah 4:6.

For a Christian it is only God Al- Mighty who helps him/her to be a successful business man/ woman and who enables him/her get the money and open the business. When a Christian gets shower of blessings from the Lord he/she have to give honour and glory to God Al-Mighty according to the Book of 1st Corinthians Chapter 10:31. Nonetheless; when a Christian gets money he/ she should not run away to manage business and lose himself/ herslf. It is great to go to heaven with a monthly income of $ 2000: 00 than to go to hell with a monthly income of $5000:00. I mention this point because many Christians are lost when they open business. When a Christian gives time to glorify the Lord it is not a waste of time. Rather it is when a Christian gives time and money that his business booms up and becomes rich according to the Book of Deuteronomy Chapter 28, Hebrews 11:40 and the Book of Isaiah 40:29-31. Any person should always be aware that money is good. But a love of money is sin.

Selected Bibliography

Anderson, Bernhard. Understanding the Old Testament. New Jersey: Prentice Hall Upper Saddle River 1998

Hershberger, Ervin. Christ in the Old Testament: Published in 1999.

Haile Selassie I, Emperor. Hiwotena Ye-Ethiopia Rimija. Addis Ababa: Birhanina Selam Printing Press 1934 Eth. Calendar

Hassen, Mekonnen. Niguse Negestu: Addis Ababa: Brana Electro Publishers 1984 Ethiopian Calendar

Helfin, Jr. Wallace. Power in Your Hand. McDougal Publishing. Hagerstown 1998.

Helfin, Jr. Wallace. Potter's House. McDougal Publishing. Hagerstown: 1998.

Spurgeon, Charles. Morning & Evening. United States Whitaker House 1997

Zewdie, Girma. Ethiopis. Addis Ababa: Nigid Matemia Dirjit 1988 Eth. Calendar